Francis Frith's
NORTH LONDON

PHOTOGRAPHIC MEMORIES

Francis Frith's
NORTH LONDON

Michael Kilburn

First published in the United Kingdom in 2000 by
Frith Book Company Ltd

Hardback Edition 2000
ISBN 1-85937-206-6

Paperback Edition 2001
ISBN 1-85937-403-4

Reprinted in Hardback 2001
ISBN 1-85937-206-6

British Library Cataloguing in Publication Data

Francis Frith's North London
Michael Kilburn

Frith Book Company Ltd
Frith's Barn, Teffont,
Salisbury, Wiltshire SP3 5QP
Tel: +44 (0) 1722 716 376
Email: info@francisfrith.co.uk
www.francisfrith.co.uk

Printed and bound in Great Britain

Contents

FRANCIS FRITH: *Victorian Pioneer*

FRANCIS FRITH, Victorian founder of the world-famous photographic archive, was a complex and fascinating man. A devout Quaker and a highly successful Victorian businessman, he was both philosophic by nature and pioneering in outlook.

By 1855 Francis Frith had already established a wholesale grocery business in Liverpool, and sold it for the astonishing sum of £200,000, which is the equivalent today of over £15,000,000. Now a multi-millionaire, he was able to indulge his passion for travel. As a child he had pored over travel books written by early explorers, and his fancy and imagination had been stirred by family holidays to the sublime mountain regions of Wales and Scotland. 'What a land of spirit-stirring and enriching scenes and places!' he had written. He was to return to these scenes of grandeur in later years to 'recapture the thousands of vivid and tender memories', but with a different purpose. Now in his thirties, and captivated by the new science of photography, Frith set out on a series of pioneering journeys to the Nile regions that occupied him from 1856 until 1860.

INTRIGUE AND ADVENTURE

He took with him on his travels a specially-designed wicker carriage that acted as both dark-room and sleeping chamber. These far-flung journeys were packed with intrigue and adventure. In his life story, written when he was sixty-three, Frith tells of being held captive by bandits, and of fighting 'an awful midnight battle to the very point of surrender with a deadly pack of hungry, wild dogs'. Sporting flowing Arab costume, Frith arrived at Akaba by camel seventy years before Lawrence, where he encountered 'desert princes and rival sheikhs, blazing with jewel-hilted swords'.

During these extraordinary adventures he was assiduously exploring the desert regions bordering the Nile and patiently recording the antiquities and peoples with his camera. He was the first photographer to venture beyond the sixth cataract. Africa was still the mysterious 'Dark Continent', and Stanley and Livingstone's historic meeting was a decade into the future. The conditions for picture taking confound belief. He laboured for hours in his wicker dark-room in the sweltering heat of the desert, while the volatile chemicals fizzed dangerously in their trays. Often he was forced to work in remote tombs and caves where conditions

were cooler. Back in London he exhibited his photographs and was 'rapturously cheered' by members of the Royal Society. His reputation as a photographer was made overnight. An eminent modern historian has likened their impact on the population of the time to that on our own generation of the first photographs taken on the surface of the moon.

VENTURE OF A LIFE-TIME

Characteristically, Frith quickly spotted the opportunity to create a new business as a specialist publisher of photographs. He lived in an era of immense and sometimes violent change. For the poor in the early part of Victoria's reign work was a drudge and the hours long, and people had precious little free time to enjoy themselves.

Most had no transport other than a cart or gig at their disposal, and had not travelled far beyond the boundaries of their own town or village. However, by the 1870s, the railways had threaded their way across the country, and Bank Holidays and half-day Saturdays had been made obligatory by Act of Parliament. All of a sudden the ordinary working man and his family were able to enjoy days out and see a little more of the world.

With characteristic business acumen, Francis Frith foresaw that these new tourists would enjoy having souvenirs to commemorate their days out. In 1860 he married Mary Ann Rosling and set out with the intention of photographing every city, town and village in Britain. For the next thirty years he travelled the country by train and by pony and trap, producing fine photographs of seaside resorts and beauty spots that were keenly bought by millions of Victorians. These prints were painstakingly pasted into family albums and pored over during the dark nights of winter, rekindling precious memories of summer excursions.

THE RISE OF FRITH & CO

Frith's studio was soon supplying retail shops all over the country. To meet the demand he gathered about him a small team of photographers, and published the work of independent artist-photographers of the calibre of Roger Fenton and Francis Bedford. In order to gain some understanding of the scale of Frith's business one only has to look at the catalogue issued by Frith & Co in 1886: it

runs to some 670 pages, listing not only many thousands of views of the British Isles but also many photographs of most European countries, and China, Japan, the USA and Canada – note the sample page shown above from the hand-written *Frith & Co* ledgers detailing pictures taken. By 1890 Frith had created the greatest specialist photographic publishing company in the world, with over 2,000 outlets – more than the combined number that Boots and WH Smith have today! The picture on the right shows the *Frith & Co* display board at Ingleton in the Yorkshire Dales. Beautifully constructed with mahogany frame and gilt inserts, it could display up to a dozen local scenes.

POSTCARD BONANZA

◆◆

The ever-popular holiday postcard we know today took many years to develop. In 1870 the Post Office issued the first plain cards, with a pre-printed stamp on one face. In 1894 they allowed other publishers' cards to be sent through the mail with an attached adhesive halfpenny stamp. Demand grew rapidly, and in 1895 a new size of postcard was permitted called the court card, but there was little room for illustration. In 1899, a year after Frith's death, a new card measuring 5.5 x 3.5 inches became the standard format, but it was not until 1902 that the divided back came into being, with address and message on one face and a full-size illustration on the other. *Frith & Co* were in the vanguard of postcard development, and Frith's sons Eustace and Cyril continued their father's monumental task, expanding the number of views offered to the public and recording more and more places in Britain, as the coasts and countryside were opened up to mass travel.

Francis Frith died in 1898 at his villa in Cannes, his great project still growing. The archive he created continued in business for another seventy years. By 1970 it contained over a third of a million pictures of 7,000 cities, towns and villages. The massive photographic record Frith has left to us stands as a living monument to a special and very remarkable man.

Frith's Archive: *A Unique Legacy*

FRANCIS FRITH'S legacy to us today is of immense significance and value, for the magnificent archive of evocative photographs he created provides a unique record of change in 7,000 cities, towns and villages throughout Britain over a century and more. Frith and his fellow studio photographers revisited locations many times down the years to update their views, compiling for us an enthralling and colourful pageant of British life and character.

We tend to think of Frith's sepia views of Britain as nostalgic, for most of us use them to conjure up memories of places in our own lives with which we have family associations. It often makes us forget that to Francis Frith they were records of daily life as it was actually being lived in the cities, towns and villages of his day. The Victorian age was one of great and often bewildering change for ordinary people, and though the pictures evoke an impression of slower times, life was as busy and hectic as it is today.

We are fortunate that Frith was a photographer of the people, dedicated to recording the minutiae of everyday life. For it is this sheer wealth of visual data, the painstaking chronicle of changes in dress, transport, street layouts, buildings, housing, engineering and landscape that captivates us so much today. His remarkable images offer us a powerful link with the past and with the lives of our ancestors.

TODAY'S TECHNOLOGY

Computers have now made it possible for Frith's many thousands of images to be accessed almost instantly. In the Frith archive today, each photograph is carefully 'digitised' then stored on a CD Rom. Frith archivists can locate a single photograph amongst thousands within seconds. Views can be catalogued and sorted under a variety of categories of place and content to the immediate benefit of researchers. Inexpensive reference prints can be created for them at the touch of a mouse button, and a wide range of books and other printed materials assembled and published for a wider, more general readership - in the next twelve months over a hundred Frith local history titles will be published! The day-to-

See Frith at www.francisfrith.co.uk

day workings of the archive are very different from how they were in Francis Frith's time: imagine the herculean task of sorting through eleven tons of glass negatives as Frith had to do to locate a particular sequence of pictures! Yet the archive still prides itself on maintaining the same high standards of excellence laid down by Francis Frith, including the painstaking cataloguing and indexing of every view.

It is curious to reflect on how the internet now allows researchers in America and elsewhere greater instant access to the archive than Frith himself ever enjoyed. Many thousands of individual views can be called up on screen within seconds on one of the Frith internet sites, enabling people living continents away to revisit the streets of their ancestral home town, or view places in Britain where they have enjoyed holidays. Many overseas researchers welcome the chance to view special theme selections, such as transport, sports, costume and ancient monuments.

We are certain that Francis Frith would have heartily approved of these modern developments, for he himself was always working at the very limits of Victorian photographic technology.

The Value of the Archive Today

Because of the benefits brought by the computer, Frith's images are increasingly studied by social historians, by researchers into genealogy and ancestory, by architects, town planners, and by teachers and schoolchildren involved in local history projects. In addition, the archive offers every one of us a unique opportunity to examine the places where we and our families have lived and worked down the years. Immensely successful in Frith's own era, the archive is now, a century and more on, entering a new phase of popularity.

The Past in Tune with the Future

Historians consider the Francis Frith Collection to be of prime national importance. It is the only archive of its kind remaining in private ownership and has been valued at a million pounds. However, this figure is now rapidly increasing as digital technology enables more and more people around the world to enjoy its benefits.

Francis Frith's archive is now housed in an historic timber barn in the beautiful village of Teffont in Wiltshire. Its founder would not recognize the archive office as it is today. In place of the many thousands of dusty boxes containing glass plate negatives and an all-pervading odour of photographic chemicals, there are now ranks of computer screens. He would be amazed to watch his images travelling round the world at unimaginable speeds through network and internet lines.

The archive's future is both bright and exciting. Francis Frith, with his unshakeable belief in making photographs available to the greatest number of people, would undoubtedly approve of what is being done today with his lifetime's work. His photographs, depicting our shared past, are now bringing pleasure and enlightenment to millions around the world a century and more after his death.

NORTH LONDON - *An Introduction*

What would-be villas, range'd in dapper pride,
Usurp the fields, and choke the highway side!
Where the prig architect, with style in view,
Has dole'd his houses forth, in two by two;
And rear's a row upon the plan, no doubt,
Of old men's jaw, with every third tooth out.

George Colman the Younger 1762–1836
'Suburbs', from 'London Rurality', 'Poetical Vagaries' 1814

THE PHOTOGRAPHS IN this volume are divided into three sections by date, rather than by location, as the time-span embraced by each section offers a self-contained view of North London at a specific and important time in its modern development.

Although Francis Frith died in 1898, his inspiration and dedication had laid the foundation upon which those coming after could build, and build they did. The task of the photographers who succeeded Frith was to set out, weighted down by the numerous accoutrements of the trade, to record in detail the everyday: not the unusual event or the artistic composition, but down-to-earth day-to-day life as it unfolded. No miniature cameras or 35mm film were to be bought in any High Street; the photographers of those days had only a rising front plate camera, a heavy wooden tripod and glass negatives which were thin and exceptionally fragile. The product of this ongoing enterprise has, at the beginning of the 21st century, furnished us with an invaluable legacy, an unsurpassed insight into a world which is long dead to us. It is a world we cannot recreate, simply because we ourselves are weighted down with the accoutrements of the 21st century; we cannot temporarily erase all that is familiar to us as early 21st-century people. Through these photographs we can come as close as it is possible to get (except perhaps through early cine footage) to entering the world of the later 19th or the early 20th century, and even the later decades of the 1950s and 1960s.

At the turn of the 20th century, Central London was a tremendously noisy, bustling hive of commerce and industry, but rightly or wrongly the vivid visual message in this first section of photographs is a certain unhurried atmosphere which pervades almost every shot. On the one hand, the photographs record views which are readily recognisable today, such as Barnet Hill, Rosslyn Hill, and Spaniards End; but on the other, here is an indelible record of areas which have changed beyond all recognition, such as Shepherds Hill, Highgate; North End, Hampstead and Stanmore Village on the Hertfordshire border.

From the early years of the century, the photographs leapfrog the first two World Wars (1914-18 and 1939-45) to record images of the years of slow economic recovery that was taking place through the 1950s. The country did not automatically right itself at the end of the Second World War, and it was a long, often depressing haul through the austerity of those post-war years into the world of the so-called 'swinging 60s'. It is easy to see that ladies' fashions did not help to cheer up the average High Street - their colours were drab and their designs were unimaginative - but at least men had for the most part cast off the ubiquitous bowler, trilby or cap, always prominent in earlier decades. The buildings in the photographs (unless destroyed or badly damaged by enemy bombing) are generally little changed from the late 1930s; thus in effect the street scenes recorded here are the street scenes of probably twenty years earlier. The street furniture, apart from some obvious exceptions, tends to fall into this same category.

By the 1960s the architectural profession was regaining its 1930s confidence; British architects were looking to America and to Europe for their inspiration. Students of architecture were not modelling themselves on their fellow countrymen; they ignored the genius of Lutyens, or even of Mendelsohn at Bexhill. Instead, they looked to Mies van de Rohe, Alvar Aalto or to Le Corbusier, in particular to his Chapel at Ronchamp, for their inspiration. It is regrettable, however, that inspiration did not play an enormous part. The architect was, in the main, to become the unwilling partner of the man or men who held the purse strings, the developer, and the country is littered with the unhappy products of this union. We do not need to look at the Bull Ring in Birmingham, or the extensive works of a single developer in Newcastle-upon-Tyne; we can look here at the backdrop to Cockfosters Underground Station, at the Commercial Development in Harrow or at Wembley Park Drive in Brent.

This volume is entitled North London, but this specific reference relates, in fact, to the Greater London of 1965. This was created when the Greater London Council, a political phoenix, rose from the ashes of the London County Council to oversee thirty-one local boroughs, along with the cities of Westminster and London. In 1986, the Conservative government under Mrs Thatcher decided in its lack of wisdom to abolish this creation, and to divert a considerable proportion of its powers to individual boroughs; each of these had its own agenda, often differing radically from that of its close neighbours. The world-renowned Historic Buildings Division of the Greater London Council was taken under the wing of English Heritage; in its hands it became a shadow of its former self. At the turn of the 21st century it appears that its so important statutory overview of the capital will soon be dealt with by the vagaries of local political whims and kiss-me-quick fancies as the reins are released. It remains to be seen, for instance, how this will affect council-owned listed buildings, particularly in Inner London boroughs; in the case of schools, for example, 'flexibility of plan' will be a key issue in the formulation of an education programme in line with current government thinking.

Apart from a single photograph (that taken in the market town of Chipping Barnet, then in Hertfordshire), these photographs were taken out and about in the ancient, now officially abolished, county of Middlesex. Abolished it may be, but it remains very much alive in its postal address, and indeed in its county cricket club; but most of all it lives on in the minds of the people who actually live in the 'county'.

As one of the smallest and oldest English counties, Middlesex has always been much under the influence of London. Occupying the north and south banks of the Thames and blending into Surrey, the South Country, it may for a brief period have comprised the Middle Saxon kingdom; but by the 8th century it had been absorbed to become a part of Mercia. With the northern part given over to forest, with marshes bordering Essex to the east, and with relatively poor agricultural soils, it failed to produce even a true county town, although Brentford had those pretentions. In effect, the county amounted only to an area of market gardens which would feed the expanding capital. In due course it became a very convenient place to build a wealthy gentleman's residence: examples are Hampton Court and Swakeleys in the west, Canons and Forty Hall in the north, and Bruce Castle in the east, not to mention Syon Park, Osterley Park, Breakspear House, Boston Manor and many more smaller houses dispersed within its boundaries.

By 1800, Enfield was the largest town in

Cockfosters, The Underground Station, Cockfosters Road c1965 C579027

Middlesex, with some 6,000 inhabitants, whereas other towns, such as Brentford and even Staines, had only one fifth that number. In fact, in the 19th century Brentford was to degenerate to such a degree that it was to become famous as one of the dirtiest and most malodorous soap-boiling towns in England, a label which it no doubt considers to be forgotten now!

By the 19th century, with railways putting relentless feelers out in the countryside, the spread of London's suburbs extended along the river to Hammersmith; villas also expanded northwards towards Hampstead and Highgate. The 1870s saw the Metropolitan District Railway open the farther reaches of the county to the attentions of speculative builders. They quickly seized upon this obvious opportunity to provide mass affordable housing for the lower middle classes, the skilled craftsmen and tradesmen. Villages such as Hendon, Finchley and Tottenham would be quickly engulfed. The early 20th century saw the London County Council building working-class estates in Hammersmith and within the inner suburban ring; the middle classes were thus pushed further into the then partial countryside, where Hornsey and Wood Green were to become classic Edwardian centres. However, it was the 1920s and 30s which were to see the great spread of suburbia. Street upon street of semi-detached houses now swamp medieval village centres in areas which until that time had remained comparatively untouched. Villages such as Ruislip, Pinner, Edgware and Stanmore have been submerged; Ruislip and Pinner managed to avoid excessive visual detriment to the village centre, but in the case of Edgware and Stanmore the developments have been totally disastrous, destroying any remnants of earlier village life.

The area encompassed in this volume is a clearly defined rectangle: it extends some fifteen miles from Ruislip in the west to Tottenham in the east, and eight miles from Wembley in the south to Enfield in the north. The focus of interest in the photographs is in the everyday world, but outside this aspect, there are multifarious rewards for the visitor. Within the 120 square mile area, ecclesiastical buildings of some note are reasonably prolific; but it is outstanding examples, such as the Church of St Lawrence, Stanmore, St Jude's, Hampstead Garden Suburb by Sir Edwin Lutyens, St Mary's, Harrow-on-the-Hill, and All Hallows, Tottenham which reward the traveller. Houses of note include Bruce Castle, Tottenham, Forty Hall, Enfield, Grovelands, Southgate and Grimsdyke, Harrow Weald; they represent a fine cross-section of gentlemanly architecture not now shut away, but visible to all. As for housing development, it is Hampstead Garden Suburb which provides an outstanding contribution to north London, while pubs such as the Salisbury, Wood Green, the Queen's Hotel, Crouch End, the King and Tinker, Enfield and the smaller Rising Sun, Mill Hill which add to the visitor's pleasure. Railway stations, many of which are architecturally distinguished, are numerous, and thus travel is relatively painless. Cinemas of note include the Gaumont State, Kilburn, the former Odeon, Rayners Lane and the presently closed and boarded-up Granada, Harrow, with its superb interior by Theodore Komisarjevsky. Theatres of quality, though rare in the area, are the Tottenham Palace, now in ecclesiastical use, and the Empire, Golders Green.

This selection of photographs serves to show how easy it is to take the familiar everyday world for granted, and to assume that the things we cherish but do not record will be available to the next generation. Wholesale clearance, for instance, is not always the enemy of the status quo; rather, it is often the imperceptible erosion of the familiar which damages a treasured townscape or landscape. The double-glazing salesmen's attack on the familiar small house, or the local council's neurotic dislike of trees, are only two examples of this continuous erosion. It is not possible to know what will remain in years to come, or what of today will come to be revered. Little built within the past two decades in this area appears to have any prospect of being treasured in the years ahead. There is no Stockley Park, Yiewsley, with its fine group of office buildings, or British Airways headquarters building near Harmondsworth to shortlist. Perhaps the smaller buildings, such as the recently-listed detached house in Aylmer Close, Stanmore, or a small group of houses in Pikes End, Eastcote, designed by a local architectural practice, which will make the grade. If grants for the repair of historic fabric finally dry up, or councils again develop the strange visions which produced the catastrophes of the late 1950s and 60s, we must wait to see whether A E Housman's sentiments will be sadly echoed in the 21st century, those feelings of loss which he expressed when he wrote:

This is the land of lost content,
I see it shining plain,
The happy highways where I went
And cannot come again.

Harrow on the Hill, Station Road 1914 66820

The Late 19th to the Early 20th Century

Forget six counties overhung with smoke
Forget the snorting steam and piston stroke,
Forget the spreading of the hideous town;
Think rather of the pack-horse on the down,
And dream of London, small, and white and clean,
The clear Thames bordered by its gardens green.

William Morris 1834–1896
'A Dream' from 'The Earthly Paradise' 1868

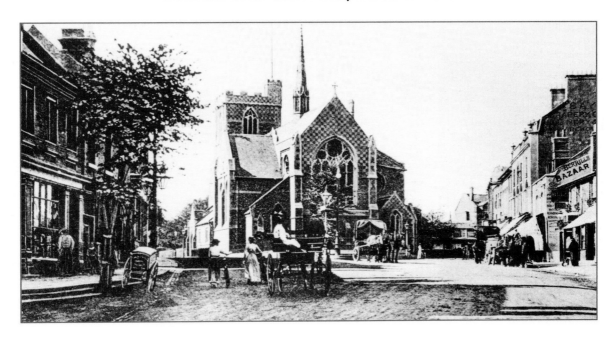

CHIPPING BARNET
Barnet Hill c1900 *B708001*
We are looking north on the approach from High Barnet Underground Station. The church of St John the Baptist dominates this readily-recognisable street scene on the crown of the hill. Early fabric in the double north aisle dates from the 15th century, but the remainder of the building was designed by William Butterfield 1875. The interior is of some interest; the Ravenscroft Chapel in the south aisle houses a fine alabaster figure of Thomas Ravenscroft, a local benefactor, dated 1630.

CROUCH END, THE BROADWAY c1890   C582302

The photograph looks from outside the present entrance to Hornsey Town Hall and towards the town centre soon after the completion of most of the buildings, and a decade before the influx of extensive but quite special Edwardian terraces. The curving parade of shops to the left, each with its well-mannered shop front, remains today. The buildings to the right of shot have long gone. Note the attractive obelisk fountain close to the foreground of the photograph.

CROUCH END, VIEW FROM SHEPHERD'S HILL c1890   C582304

This photograph exudes the atmosphere of well-manicured countryside. It was taken literally weeks before the start of the building of a series of individual, sometimes rather grand villas, which were to extend from the heights of Highgate Hill to Crouch End. It remains an extraordinarily well-preserved and pleasing area to wander in on a sunny spring afternoon.

CROUCH END
Crouch End Hill c1890 C582301
Look up the hill at the turn of the century, and see this posed but
superbly evocative photograph of an attractive mixture of domestic
building styles, culminating in the spire of Blomfield's Christ
Church. Here is the three-storey flat-fronted brick house of the
later 18th century, small bungalow shops added to two-storey
houses of various dates, and to the left the utility weather-boarding
above the barber's shop.

FINCHLEY, NEW TOWN c1890 F64301

This is a classic photograph of a north London suburb around the turn of the century, with a mix of design and scale in the road-side buildings. Shop fronts with their windows bulging with merchandise, and a certain unhurried atmosphere, present a picture of life far removed from the mobile 'phone and computerised urgency of the early 21st century.

HAMPSTEAD, ROSSLYN HILL 1898 41583

The camera looks towards Hampstead High Street, formerly Red Lion Hill. The mid 19th-century houses are fairly run-of-the-mill, but had the cameraman turned round he could have photographed a fairly new arrival on the Hill. This is St Stephen's Church, designed by S S Teulon in 1873, a superb red-brick High Victorian building. It has suffered gravely since being declared redundant in 1977, and is boarded up at the time of writing. The church is included in English Heritage's Register of Buildings at Risk in Greater London.

HAMPSTEAD HEATH
The Heath from Parliament Hill 1898 41600
The Heath, extending from Kenwood House in the north to an
area around Parliament Hill in the south, occupies some 800 acres;
it has been popular with artists and authors (and the Gordon
Rioters) since the 18th century. The photograph contrasts fenced
and hedged sheep pastures with visual echoes of heathland. The
spired church of St Anne Brookfield, 1853, by George Plunkett, is
clearly seen silhouetted against the sky, with St Joseph's, more
familiarly known as 'Holy Joe's', to its right. The view has altered
dramatically in one hundred years - a mass of buildings has sprung
up on the facing hill slope, and the Heath has become literally a
wooded park with lakes.

HAMPSTEAD, HIGH STREET 1898 41570
The camera looks from the High
Street towards Holly Hill, and on
towards West Heath. The simple but
somehow graceful shop fronts have
gone, although the buildings remain,
including the Old Fire Station of 1873,
with its prominent tower. It is
regrettable that its original use has
been supplanted by offices, and that
the upper part of the tower above the
clock has been removed. One day,
perhaps with the help of a small grant,
this may be properly rebuilt, but the
passing of the wonderful street
furniture is almost certainly forever.

HAMPSTEAD HEATH, THE BATHING POND 1898 41590
This is the more subdued face of the Heath the shot is not packed with action. The ponds have for many years been used for swimming, fishing and sailing model craft. The area is much grown up now, and a fine wildlife preserve.

HAMPSTEAD HEATH, ST STEPHEN'S FROM THE POND 1898 41589
St Stephen's Church is prominent on Rosslyn Hill above the tranquil water of the pond, which is disturbed only by a few fishermen and rather more observers.

HAMPSTEAD HEATH, THE VIADUCT AND THE POND 1898 41587
The five-arch later 19th-century red-brick bridge still rather pompously carries a narrow roadway across the pond in the south west angle of the Heath. The banks are grown up now with immature trees and undergrowth, rendering the overall setting rather more romantic. It is a pity that the stone balustrade has given way to a plain iron railing.

HAMPSTEAD HEATH, WHITE STONE POND 1898 41592
Superficially, little has changed. A large building continues to form a backdrop to the scene, but it is regrettable that it is now a rather harsh block of flats known as Summit Lodge. Only a fragment of the original boundary wall remains in Judges Walk.

HAMPSTEAD, NORTH END 1898 41579
Not much more than a stone's throw from Jack Straw's Castle, the original Old Bull and Bush can be seen on the right of shot. The road at the foot of the hill still curves past the pub, but the houses adjacent to Sandy Close, to the left, have been rebuilt. The road is wider and most of the trees have gone.

HAMPSTEAD HEATH, THE OLD BULL AND BUSH, NORTH END ROAD 1898 41581
The pub is said to have been built as a farm in the mid 17th century, and it was licensed in 1721. It is alleged to have been the house of William Hogarth, the painter. Among its known drinkers were Thomas Gainsborough, Joshua Reynolds and David Garrick. The building seen in the photograph appears as an atmospheric drinkers' dream pub, with its low doorway stepping down into a dark panelled bar, with its inevitably yellowy-brown smoke-stained ceiling.

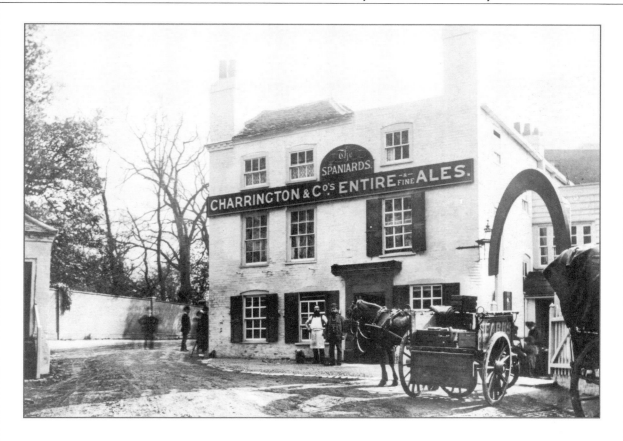

HAMPSTEAD HEATH
The Spaniards, Spaniards End 1890 H391095
Said to have been founded by the Spanish Ambassador's valet, the
18th-century pub, with its adjacent toll house, formed the entrance
to the Bishop of London's Hornsey estate. Little in the view has
drastically altered. The semi-circular arch has gone from what is
now the car park entrance, and the rather fine pub sign has also
disappeared. The pinch-point in the road caused the local council
to toy with the idea of demolishing the listed Toll House in the
1970s, but local views were listened to and it remains today. Behind
the pub is Evergreen Hill, the home of Henrietta Barnet, the
founder of Hampstead Garden Suburb.

HAMPSTEAD HEATH, SPANIARDS ROAD 1898 41595

Taken from close to the Spaniards pub, this view looks along the dead straight link between North End Way and Hampstead Lane, which is still recognisable. Extensive tree cover dropping away onto the Heath now obscures the raised footway, which remains extant, and inevitably a kerb now defines the right-hand side of the road.

HARROW ON THE HILL, ST MARY'S CHURCH, CHURCH HILL 1906 55673

Prominent for many miles, St Mary's has dominated the hill since at least the 12th century. It has always been an extremely important church as a peculiar of the Archbishop of Canterbury. Although quite heavily 'restored' by Sir George Gilbert Scott in 1849, the building retains much original fabric, including glass by Kempe and Comper, and memorials by Flaxman and Scheemakers. A particularly striking monument is that by Humphrey Hopper to John North, who died in 1831, which occupies a space adjacent to the north door.

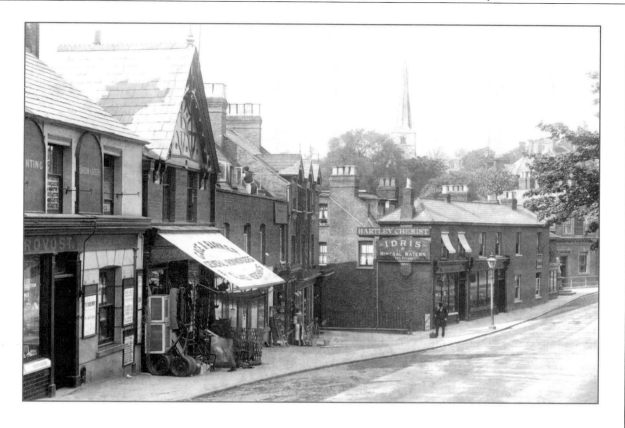

HARROW ON THE HILL
High Street 1906 53630

This photograph was taken from almost exactly the same viewpoint as one to be seen later taken in 1960; it is very much apparent that at this time the village was a thriving, almost self-sufficient commercial centre. Virtually every building has a shop front, but today the number is considerably reduced, and their uses are less practical - for instance, Hartley Chemist is now a restaurant. Many other shops have disappeared from the hill as dormitory residents opt for the under-one-roof convenience of the local supermarkets.

The withdrawal of shopping from the village is not a recent phenomenon; in fact, it began prior to the First World War, when the shops on the western slope became houses, leaving only their large windows as evidence of an earlier use.

HARROW ON THE HILL, STATION ROAD 1914 66820
Here we see a simple, well-proportioned range of three-storey shops and flats of around 1890, with their fine sensitively-crafted pilastered fronts. The photographs revives memories of old friends such as the Home and Colonial Stores, now sadly departed, and of the days when fascia lettering reflected a firm's pride in itself and its products. It is rather surprising that most of the buildings in the shot have survived, although generally in a down-graded form. The bushes on the right have gone, to be replaced by shops.

HARROW ON THE HILL
High Street and Church Hill 1906 53638

The camera looks north, with Old Schools on the left; this is effectively the original Harrow School building of 1608, with the wing seen here added by C R Cockerell in 1819. Much of the original interior remains, including timber panelling heavily inscribed by former pupils, including Byron, Sheridan and Winston Churchilll. To the right is the Gothic school chapel of 1854 designed by Sir George Gilbert Scott, while further to the right, but out of shot, is the library of 1861, also by Scott, and recently sensitively re-ordered by local architect Andrew Reed. All-in-all, it is a picturesque group. Further down the hill can be seen the speech rooms by William Burges.

HARROW ON THE HILL, THE OLD SCHOOLS, CHURCH HILL 1914 66815
Apart from the demolition of the late 18th-century house, in the centre, little has changed visually. The original panelled school room is housed in the ground floor of the left-hand wing, while behind the prominent high bay window is a modern school museum. Extensive work was recently carried out to repair and restore the badly decayed bell turret which crowns Old Schools.

HARROW ON THE HILL, GENERAL VIEW, SOUTH WEST 1906 53629
The slopes to the rear of West Street are still green, and the view at the end of the 20th century is a little less smoke-hazed. The Fives Courts in the left foreground of the photograph are a bit dilapidated, but they are now roofed; the adjacent Gymnasium Building is little altered. The big change is the addition, in the lee of the hill, of a well-designed theatre block by Kenneth W Reed and Associates of Harrow, along with a number of equally well-designed houses.

HARROW ON THE HILL, VIEW WEST FROM WATFORD ROAD 1906 55670

This view has stood the test of time, and the visitor today would see little apparent change. St Mary's Church dominates the photograph from its well-treed setting, with to its right the sheer elevation of The Foss and Grove Hill by Habershon, and to its left the Speech Room tower and chapel fleché.

HARROW ON THE HILL, PETERBOROUGH ROAD 1906 53634

It all looks neater now, and the trees have been thinned. Nothing new architecturally has been added. Clearly visible in the photograph is the Old Music School, now replaced lower on the slope by a grander building by E S Prior. Behind the trees, with only the chimney pots visible, are the purpose-built school houses, Garlands, The Knoll and Hillside. Football Lane runs sharply downhill to the right. Behind the camera, built into the boundary wall, is a small stone plaque commemorating, what may well have been Britain's first fatal motor accident.

HARROW ON THE HILL
Deynecourt, Harrow Park 1906

Harrow Park winds away to the east of the High Street, past one or two rather grand houses, to arrive at Deynecourt at the foot of the hill. Carefully positioned, with views to the north over School Lake, this is an imposing Italianate house with fine red brick and terra cotta facing, accessed by an imposing triple-arch porte-cochere. Search the high bank on the opposite side of the road and find remnants of a Gothic folly which once ornamented the grounds of The Park.

◆

STANMORE
The Village 1906

Here are buildings of the second half of the 19th century, with an object lesson to be observed in the treatment of boundary walls and railings - all neat and carefully designed. All has gone now to make way for the less-than-sparkling commercial centre of today - it was once a centre of character, but now basically a characterless centre.

HARROW ON THE HILL, DEYNECOURT, HARROW PARK 1906 53641

STANMORE, THE VILLAGE 1906 55692

STANMORE

Old Church, Uxbridge Road 1906 55695

Great and Little Stanmore are situated close to the Hertfordshire
border, and it is to the rising ground above the present village that
the visitor needs to look for semi-rural quality. Up here is Bentley
Priory, remodelled by Sir John Soane in the late 18th century,
where Queen Adelaide died in 1849; here, too, is Stanmore Hall, a
remarkable ragstone building which until a great conflagration in
1979 housed a sumptuous William Morris interior. At the foot of
the hill the Old Church and St John the Evangelist share a single
churchyard, while remnants of the original mediaeval parish
church can be found to the south.

◆

STANMORE
The Church of St John the Evangelist, Uxbridge Road 1906

To the east of the Old Church, but sharing its graveyard, is the Church of St John The Evangelist. The view of this ragstone building, designed by Henry Clutton in 1894, has changed very little. Close to the buttress nearest the camera, W S Gilbert, of Gilbert and Sullivan fame, sleeps under the widespread wings of a white angel; Gilbert lived at Grimsdyke, a house by Norman Shaw, to the north. Inside the church, which is very rarely open, are the monuments saved from the Old Church - they are well worth seeing.

◆

STANMORE
The Village 1906

In thirty years, this scene would be reinterpreted to become the Broadway. Gone would be the village pump, the pond and the water splash. Gone the row of cottages, probably only thirty years old when the photograph was taken, and now gone is the Red House, an 18th-century building behind its boundary wall, but out of sight to the extreme right of the photograph. Behind the pump can be seen a row of early 17th-century plastered, timber-framed cottages, said to possess the longest unbroken jetty in Greater London.

STANMORE, THE CHURCH OF ST JOHN THE EVANGELIST, UXBRIDGE ROAD 1906 55693

STANMORE, THE VILLAGE 1906 55691

**STANMORE,
THE VILLAGE 1906** 55690
The village is now a faceless sort of
place, apart from one or two buildings;
these include a superb but well-
disguised hall house of around 1500 in
Church Road. In the main, the village
now lacks either grace or inspiration in
its buildings; to some extent, relief can
be gained at its western end through
the high-walled Bernays Gardens, a few
houses around Old Church Lane, and
the two adjacent churches.

**TOTTENHAM,
LORDSHIP LANE 1903** T300343
This view looks east towards the
junction of Lordship Lane and Bruce
Grove. The open area to the left is the
site of the yet to be built Peabody
Housing Estate and in the right
foreground is the corner of Mount
Pleasant Road. Bruce Castle Park can
be seen just beyond the trees. This is
an interesting shot, taken at that
moment when the area was being
transformed from the semi-rural into
a full-blown Edwardian suburb.

The 1950s

Where herbs did grow
And flowers sweet
But now 'tis called
Saint Georges Street.

Finch's Grotto, a pleasure garden in Southwark, was destroyed by fire in 1775, and a road was built over the ashes. The sentiment expressed by a local poet could well have been addressed to villages such as Edgware in the 1930s and on into the later 50s.

BURNT OAK, EDGWARE ROAD c1955 B706011
Burnt Oak will never be at the cutting edge of the tourist industry, but as we look north towards Edgware, we can see that the buildings on the left of this view are of some interest. Designed in the 1930s with enough imagination to take them away from the general run of Neo-Georgian buildings in the area, they are decorated with lion masks and finished with a decorative cavetto cornice. We can also see a good selection of contemporary cars.

BURNT OAK, EDGWARE ROAD c1955 B706009
Development came to Burnt Oak in the early 1920s with the arrival of the Northern Line. Although the buildings to the extreme left and right of the photograph are little changed apart from their shop fronts, the Gaumont Cinema has gone, making space for an unattractive supermarket. Hidden behind the long block to the right is The Broadway, a not unattractive pantiled pub. Other buildings further on have been demolished.

BURNT OAK, EDGWARE ROAD c1955 B706007
This view has hardly changed in forty-five years. The buildings are almost an oasis amongst giant office blocks, car sales lots, and showrooms.

BURNT OAK, WATLING AVENUE c1955 B706006
Watling Avenue buzzes with activity. Street traders do good business, and upmarket shops, such as Dorothy Perkins, are willing to occupy comparatively small units. Dorothy Perkins has gone now, and the street seems to have lost its commercial edge.

BURNT OAK, WATLING AVENUE c1955 B706012
A cyclist gingerly crosses Edgware Road as Watling Avenue drops away eastwards towards Mill Hill. Apart from a sign of the times - the bank building on the left has given way to an amusement arcade - little has physically changed.

BUSH HILL
Elmscott Gardens, c1955 B870015

Look carefully at the unified appearance of this cul-de-sac as it
backs onto Bush Hill Golf course. Look at the everyday houses
which not long ago were taken for granted, and even ridiculed as
semi-detached suburbia. Look at the timber windows with their
coloured glass, the original front doors, the solid, yet attractive,
garage doors, the original gates and boundary walls, and realise
that all this has for the greater part disappeared. Unaltered pairs of
such houses do exist, but most have received the treatment meted
out at the hands of the double-glazing salesman and the need to
park that extra car in the front garden. Look carefully at these
houses, and then look about you forty-five years on. Soon they may
be listed as rare architectural survivals.

COLINDALE, EDGWARE ROAD c1955 C580008

Said to derive its name from a local family, the area basically occupies a stretch of Edgware Road about a mile south of Edgware. Wakemans Hill Parade, dated 1931, sets an acceptable design standard at this date, but this has now to a greater extent been supplanted by modern offices and industrial estate architecture in the area. Almost out of shot, the severe faience-fronted former Odeon has ceased to show films.

EASTCOTE, ST LAWRENCE'S CHURCH, BRIDLE ROAD c1955 E178004

Until around the outbreak of the First World War, Eastcote was a part of Ruislip parish, and it was in 1913 that the Bishop of London's Fund purchased land and a Mission Church was built. Additional land followed; after what appears to have been some behind-the-scenes 'discussions', the architect Charles Nicholson was appointed in 1932 to design the present attractive and well-detailed brick-faced building. Particularly pleasant is the Tuscan-columned interior, with its round arches under a wagon roof.

EDGWARE, STATION ROAD c1955 E126007

Half close your eyes, and it is almost possible to visualise village Edgware. Visit today, and see that the pub has gone, and that offices and shops of little architectural merit have come to dominate the street scene. If you should pass this way, take time to reflect on the dignified, simple memorial to two children who died at Aberfan on 21 October 1956, victims of a disaster which should never have happened; it is situated close to the western churchyard entrance gate, which can be seen in the photograph.

EDGWARE, ST MARGARET'S CHURCH, STATION ROAD c1955 E126023

The trees have grown, and the street signs have changed, but the church, with its substantial 15th-century ragstone west tower and mid 18th-century brick-faced body, remains substantially unaltered behind its panelled brick boundary wall. The church is close to the main road and vulnerable to vandalism, so access is rarely easy; but the interior, whilst not of breathtaking interest, is worth seeing.

EDGWARE, THE RAILWAY HOTEL, STATION ROAD c1955 E126003

Between the underground station and the parish church, this is a wonderful neo-Tudor pub of 1936 by A E Sewell; he also designed the Crown and Anchor in High Street, Chipping Barnet, and the Goat near Forty Hill, Enfield, in the same style for the brewers Truman, Hanbury and Buxton. Detail, both internally and externally, is paramount, from the clustered brick chimney stacks to the beautifully-carved brackets supporting the jettying. It is a great pity that the off-sales wing, seen here to the right of the main building, has for some time been in a shabby rundown condition.

EDGWARE, THE UNDERGROUND STATION, STATION ROAD c1955 E126028

This is an unusual but very attractive station at the end of the Northern Line, designed by Stanley Heaps in 1924; at the time he was architect to the London Underground Electric Railways. With its paired columns and pantiled roofs, the station shares its friendly feel with C W Clarks' smaller station at Stanmore of 1932.

**EDGWARE,
STATION ROAD c1955** E126032
Station Road is readily recognisable as it drops away from the underground station towards Hale Lane and Mill Hill. It is sad that the essentially 1930s character of the shop fronts has been eroded away by plate glass and aluminium. It cannot be said that the buildings are architecturally exciting, but they do express the solid confidence of the 1930s Outer London suburbs.

EDGWARE, STATION ROAD FROM EDWAREBURY LANE c1955 E126009
Dated 1923, the neo-Georgian terrace of shops and flats was built to coincide with the arrival of the Northern Line in that same year. The reassuring style of the architecture, with its Ionic pilasters and solid timber and glass shop fronts, was designed to attract the young city worker to live in a world somewhere between the town and the country. Out of shot to the left is a very pretty bank building in the same, but rather more luxurious, style.

EDGWARE, EDGWAREBURY LANE c1955 E126026
This is probably the most dull row of buildings in Edgware town. Romantically titled King's Parade, it is sited at the southern end of Edgwarebury Lane as it strikes north to cross open farmland at Edgware Bury, and on to Elstree. Since the photograph was taken an additional length of ten windows has been added to replace the more decorative advertisement hoardings.

EDGWARE
High Street c1955 E126034
The High Street, which forms part of the Roman Watling Street, has been devastated by road widening in the 1930s. Early photographs show a village of timber-framed buildings, of which a few survive, all on the west side of the road; they include a very fine 16th-century hall house and a range of timber-framed houses, now shops. The grey, granite war memorial in memory of the fallen of 1914-1918, with its rough-hewn finish, dominates the photograph; immediately behind is a small free-standing building which, although constructed around the 1930s, gained the distinction of reputedly being the blacksmith's shop upon which Handel based his 'Harmonious Blacksmith'.

EDGWARE
George V Memorial Gardens,
Canons Park, Canons Drive c1955 E126020
Originally owned by the Priory of St Bartholomew The Great, the
estate was acquired in 1709 by James Brydges, later Duke of
Chandos. Here he created one of London's great houses. After the
Duke's death the estate was sold and the house demolished; various
features were salvaged and dispersed, mainly over southern
England. The present building on its site, now the North London
Collegiate School, dates from 1910, and it is difficult to say with
absolute certainty whether any of the original fabric is incorporated
in the structure. Handel was Kapellmeister here between 1717 and
1719, and wrote the eleven Chandos Anthems for his patron. He is
said to have played the organ at one of the most amazing churches
in Greater London, St Lawrence, Whitchurch Lane. Two walled
gardens that once belonged to the house survive, including the
Memorial Gardens, which were laid out in 1938.

ENFIELD, CHURCH STREET c1955 E179002

Situated on its northern edge, Enfield is one of the most attractive market towns within the Greater London area; it was well-established by Domesday. Not a wealthy town until the arrival of the railway in 1849, it has now become irretrievably linked to Central London by a 1930s sea of suburbia. This photograph looks eastwards towards the mediaeval town centre, but apart from reminding us that shop fascias were once sensitively designed, and that shopping streets were once pedestrian-friendly, the view is not flattering.

ENFIELD, THE TOWN c1955 E179004

Close to the northern end of London Road, the market place and the parish church, the weatherboarded Ebben Steam Bakery, now departed, contributes to the market town feel of the photograph. Although it is as well-designed as a high rise building can be in a small-scale setting, the twelve-storey Civic Centre lurks menacingly just round the corner in Silver Street.

ENFIELD,
THE MARKET PLACE c1955 E179003
The compact market place on the north side of the town is enhanced by its octagonal timber market cross, built in 1903 in celebration of Edward VII's coronation to replace a stone Gothic cross of 1826. The earlier cross was moved to the gardens of Myddleton House at Bulls Cross. Burtons is a fine example of its genre, while the flank elevation of the Rialto Cinema enhances neither its neighbouring buildings nor the market place as a whole.

ENFIELD, THE OPEN AIR SWIMMING POOL c1955
E179023

A natural progression maybe from the 19th-century enclosed public baths and wash-houses, Lidos sprang up in the 1930s all around London. It is regrettable that their popularity died as aquatic requirements became more sophisticated; many have disappeared completely, or lie dormant - for instance, the recently-listed Uxbridge Lido, and Ruislip, where the buildings have been reduced to pub use. In the face of vastly expensive fitness centres, it is highly unlikely that such a phenomenon will be seen again.

GOLDERS GREEN, FINCHLEY ROAD c1955 G271010
The camera looks north across the Golders Green
Road/North End Road crossing. The view is
dominated by a very attractive shopping parade by
Welch and Hollis of 1913, and beyond somewhat
utilitarian premises of the 1930s looks on towards
Hampstead Garden Suburb; this was said by Nikolaus
Pevsner to be 'the aesthetically most satisfactory and
socially most successful of all 20th-century garden
suburbs'. To visit Golders Green without extending
that visit to the Suburb is to deprive oneself of an
exciting architectural experience.

**ENFIELD, BUSH HILL PARK,
ST MARKS ROAD c1955** E179036
One stop down the line from Enfield town, Bush Hill
Park station was opened in 1880 to service this
development by the Northern Estates Company. The
grand pub and the simple working men's houses and
shops in St Marks Road and First Avenue are all of a
similar date. Beyond the featureless station wall, the
more up-market buildings of Queen Annes Place
and Dryden Road can be seen. Close by, in Private
Road, is a house of some architectural significance
designed in the Arts and Crafts manner by Arthur
Macmurdo for his brother.

HAMPSTEAD HEATH
Jack Straw's Castle, North End Way c1955 H391004
The pub occupies a picturesque setting on the crown of the hill,
and is named after the leader of the Peasants' Revolt of 1381. The
photograph shows what remained after the pub was badly damaged
by Second World War bombing. The brick building on the left
remains in situ, but the remainder was rebuilt to the designs of
Raymond Erith in 1964, on a giant scale, in a weather-boarded
Gothic style. The obelisk has now been removed to a safer position
at the roadside. Behind the fence on the extreme right is Heath
House, an attractive building of the later 18th century.

HAMPSTEAD HEATH
The Old Bull and Bush, North End Road c1955 H391011
The earlier pub on the site, made famous by the music
hall star Florrie Ford, was demolished in the early 1920s,
and rebuilt to a vaguely similar design. The bay windows
of the old pub are echoed by sashed windows above, but
the new brick-faced building is inescapably of its period.
Internally, some old features have been retained, and
there are good inter-war fittings as well. Note the
retention of the sphinx-like figures on the copings at
either end of the central bay.

◆

HENDON,
WATFORD WAY c1955 H397026
Hendon was first recorded in the 10th century, but the Hendon we see in this photograph has very little in common with the original mediaeval centre about half a mile (as the crow flies) to the north. The expansion we see here was directly associated with a major road link into London and the arrival of the Northern Line in 1923. The neo-Georgian buildings around Central Circus clearly reflect that date, with the somewhat faceless super-cinema following a decade or so later. Enjoy the street furniture in this photograph, which includes a now almost-forgotten item - a police-box.

HENDON, VIVIAN AVENUE c1955 H397022
The western arm of Central Circus and the thin neo-Georgian buildings are not architecturally distinguished. There is some interest to be found in the parade of 1950s fashions and transport of the day.

KINGSBURY, THE SWIMMING POOL, KINGSBURY ROAD c1955 K142054
The Kingsbury pool was large by municipal standards, and it was situated on the edge of Roe Green Park. The Art Deco buildings were elegant and stream-lined, but along with so many other outdoor pools all over Britain it has been demolished; this is partly due to an ever-decreasing interest, but perhaps mainly through the advent of the oh-so-comfortable fitness centre.

KINGSBURY, STATION PARADE, KINGSBURY ROAD c1950 K142012

It has to be said that Kingsbury is an area of contrasts. Hardly a stone's throw away from Kingsbury Road is Slough Lane and its environs, where Ernest G Trobridge's timber and thatch houses are grouped most picturesquely. A pioneer in the use of green elm, Trobridge experimented with this patented building system, but with a singular lack of success. Back in more mundane Kingsbury Road, Station Parade, with its paper-thin symmetry and air of parsimony sets the mercenariness of suburban development before us.

MILL HILL, THE BROADWAY c1955 M357003

Arts and Crafts-style buildings, and the churches of St Michael and All Angels and the Sacred Heart and St Mary Immaculate set the pace and quality at this new Mill Hill, away from the old centre but close to the railway. A reminder of the area's agrarian ancestry is to be found in Goodwyn Avenue, where the early 18th-century Lawrence Farmhouse stands, now indifferently converted to offices.

MILL HILL, THE KING'S ARMS PUB, STIRLING CORNER c1955 M357015
Well-designed bollards and street signs front a typical road-house at the junction of the Great North Road with the lesser east-west Elstree to Chipping Barnet Road. It is difficult not to feel a certain nostalgia for this grassy, almost rural roundabout.

MILL HILL, THE GOLF CLUB, BARNET WAY c1955 M357017
Look south away from Stirling Corner and past Mill Hill Golf Club bordering Thistle Wood and Scratch Wood (a rural name now adopted by the local motorway service station), and take a moment to reflect on a pre-dual carriageway Great North Road. There are tree-lined verges of considerable width, and two or three cars and cyclists little knowing the madness of dual carriageway traffic engineering that is just around the corner.

PINNER, HIGH STREET c1955 P296010

Pinora, recorded in the Feet of Fines in 1232, is a village of considerable beauty and well-manicured charm. The church of St John The Baptist, whose tower dominates the rising High Street, appears to date from the 13th century. In the church tower close to the south porch is a most eccentric monument erected by J C Louden to the memory of his parents. Under the church tower can be seen the former Hilltop Wine Bar, its fake timbering hiding a good example of 17th-century framing, while to the left of the tower is a fine house by Sir Ernest George. In the village lived Horatia Nelson, daughter of Admiral Lord Nelson and Lady Emma Hamilton. She now lies buried in the local cemetery in Paines Lane under a simple stone surround.

PINNER, HIGH STREET c1955 P296002

This photograph was taken from the junction of the High Street with Bridge Street. The dominant buildings are of the early 1900s, complete with a fine set of chimney stacks. To the right is a rather shabby jettied 16th-century pub, which, it must be said, has been repaired and redecorated in latter years. The remainder of the buildings have changed little, including an excellent early 18th-century brick-fronted house halfway up the hill.

PINNER, BRIDGE STREET C1955 P296012

As we look at this mundane street as it drops down towards Pinner Underground Station, under the railway bridge and on towards Harrow-on-the-Hill, there is little to herald the wonderful surprise of turning into the High Street just beyond the bland buildings of the 1950s. Take time to absorb the area, including Moss Lane, Church Lane, Paines Lane and, of course, the High Street.

PRESTON, PRESTON ROAD C1955 P381024

The Red Book of the Exchequer, 1212, records Prestone, meaning the enclosure of the priests, but this romantic derivation is little evidenced here in the heart of commuter-land. The station was opened in 1932 in this row of emaciated Arts and Crafts buildings. All-in-all, the cars in the photograph are of greater visual interest.

RUISLIP
Bury Street c1955 R335038

The Village Sweet Shop and Hailey's have gone, and this very pretty building, which hides a 17th-century timber frame behind its brick skin, is now a restaurant, to which has been added a not very beautiful plastic conservatory. Note the fine heavy chimney stack. The cottages are now shops, but the timber-framed gabled range adjacent remains in residential use. On the north side of the village is Manor Farm, with its astonishingly complete array of farm buildings. A motte and bailey castle, complete with its outer bailey and extensive village outworks, define the origins of the settlement. However, it is the buildings within the earthworks which deserve comment and inspection: these include the Great Barn of the 13th century, probably the oldest timber structure in Middlesex, the library, a 17th-century conversion, the cow byre (somewhat renewed after several arson attacks) and the Farmhouse, a quite complex fragment of the 17th century. The buildings are presently in the ownership of the London Borough of Hillingdon, who recently turned away at the last moment from a resolution to market the buildings - a potential disaster put in the pending tray.

◆

RUISLIP, HIGH STREET c1955 R335020

This view looks north. The High Street, fashioned in the 1930s, drops down to the original village centre, with the graveyard to St Martins church on the immediate right. In the graveyard is a fine tomb, which was recently listed, in the style of Eric Gill. Ruislip, or 'wet place', is, like Pinner, engulfed in 1930s semi-detached metroland, but even here surprises are to be had. Not many years ago, in an unprepossessing house off the High Street, a timber-framed building of the 17th century was found, quite by accident, wrapped in its 1930s brick overcoat.

SOUTHGATE, HIGH STREET AND THE BOURNE c1955 S641080

Close to the underground station are two major historic buildings. Behind the high brick wall to the extreme right of the photograph is Southgate House of the late 18th century, built in the form of a neo-classical villa by Samuel Pole; a short distance along the Bourne is Grovelands, a beautiful house designed by John Nash in 1797, and still within its own park, which has connections to Repton. In the 1980s there was considerable concern for the future of this house, but as if in the nick of time it was bought, restored and converted to hospital use. The price tag for the restoration was a fairly large addition to the building, but this has weathered in well. Grovelands achieved a certain notoriety in the late 1990s by playing host to General Pinochet.

SOUTHGATE, CHASE SIDE C1950 S641009
Later 19th-century buildings can be seen in the photograph extending along Chase Side, and away towards Cockfosters, but it is the building on the extreme right which catches the eye. Its shop front, and indeed its whole demeanour, almost shout reliability and good solid service. Unfortunately, flashy cuckoos have taken over the High Street nest.

WHETSTONE, HIGH ROAD AND THE BLACK BULL PUB C1955 W480016
It would be difficult to say now, without consulting early maps, exactly where 18th-century Whetstone began and finished on the Great North Road. The photograph shows an area to the south of the original village as it drops down towards Tally Ho Corner, but just a little to the north, among the modern shops, are 18th-century houses and a fine 16th-century timber-framed building - an interesting piece of townscape archaeology.

The 1960s

By seeing London, I have seen as much of life as the world can show.

James Boswell 1740–1794
'Tour of the Hebrides' 1773

COCKFOSTERS
Christ Church, Chalk Lane c1965 C579026
Designed by Henry Edward Kendall in 1839, and situated to the west of Cockfosters Underground station, this stock brick church was financed by the Bevan family who owned Trent Park, and whose origins were linked to Quaker traditions. The building has echoes of the Commissioners' preaching boxes so familiar around London, but in 1898 this austere quality was partly ameliorated by additions to the designs of Sir Arthur Blomfield.

COCKFOSTERS, THE UNDERGROUND STATION, COCKFOSTERS ROAD c1965 C579027

Simply elegant, this is the last of a superb series of 1930s underground stations extending along the northern section of the Piccadilly Line, including Arnos Grove, Southgate and Oakwood, all designed by the master of proportion and style, Charles Holden. The long, low concrete-canopied entrance drops to an airy clerestoried train shed, which, in turn, compliments that at Uxbridge, the western terminus on the line, designed by the same architect. Try to ignore the curving backdrop building.

COCKFOSTERS, HEDDON COURT PARADE, COCKFOSTERS ROAD c1965 C579016

Situated a short distance to the south of the underground station, this archetypal 1930s parade of shops and flats sits comfortably with it and its well-treed and manicured surroundings. Until the arrival of the Piccadilly Line in 1933, Cockfosters was little more than a rural hamlet, and even now it is on the very northern edge of London as it extends out into Enfield Chase.

COCKFOSTERS
Trent Park, (Middlesex University) c1965 C579006
Enclosed from Enfield Chase in 1777, and acquired by royal
physician Sir Richard Jebb, Trent Park covered some two hundred
acres. The present red-brick house supersedes the much smaller
original one designed for Jebb by Sir William Chambers; although
it is large, with re-used features salvaged from other demolished
London buildings, it is not exciting. Now the campus of Middlesex
University, the whole has taken on a care-worn air, which even
extends to the early 18th-century garden statues by John van Nost,
which were brought to the house by Sir Philip Sassoon from Stowe
in Buckinghamshire. The statues are included in the English
Heritage Register of Buildings at Risk in London.

COCKFOSTERS, TRENT PARK, THE SWIMMING POOL c1965 C579004
To the east of the house, the swimming pool, with its red-brick orangery designed by Reginald Cooper in the mid 1930s, presents a peaceful well-ordered scene. This is a small part of an extensive improvement scheme initiated and implemented by Sir Philip Sassoon, the third Baronet, which was continued until his death in 1939.

COLINDALE, EDGWARE ROAD c1960 C580021
The widening of the A5 (Watling Street) removed a number of buildings of late mediaeval and later dates, particularly as it passed through Edgware. Colindale was hardly developed until it became associated with aircraft production during the First World War, and with nearby Hendon Aerodrome, which was developed by its then owner, the aircraft pioneer Claude Grahame-White. His hangar, which dates from 1915, is included in English Heritage's Register of Buildings at Risk in London.

CROUCH END
The Broadway, Looking North c1965 C582004
This area was called Crouche in 1400; the name derives from Old
English 'cruc' or cross, but does this mean cross-roads or near to
the cross? It is a rarity among North London centres in that it
stands well away from underground and railway stations, which may
or may not account for the survival of such very fine groups of late
19th-century and Edwardian buildings as fill this photograph. The
quirky terracotta and brick Clock Tower was designed by F G
Knight 1805. Crouch End possesses two of London's outstanding
late 19th-century pubs, the Queens Hotel and the Salisbury.

CROUCH END, THE BROADWAY c1965 C582007

The road drops down into the Broadway with an array of modest but attractive late 19th- and early 20th-century buildings. What can be said in defence of the intruder on the right of the photograph? Very little!

CROUCH END, THE BROADWAY c1965 C582006

This photograph was taken from close to the site of the obelisk fountain which is visible in the photograph taken in c1890. The curving parade remains little altered in 1965, but already shop fronts are becoming gaudy and fascias oversized. On the right is a glimpse of the electricity showrooms which bound the open frontage to the Town Hall on its north side, while to the south are the gas showrooms.

CROUCH END
Christ Church, Crouch End Hill c1965
Standing high above the town centre and attractively sited on the crown of the hill, the church with its elegant broach spire was designed by Sir Arthur Blomfield in c1861, but not completed until 1881, when the west porch was added. Although the exterior is faced in Kentish ragstone, the interior is of somewhat more mundane brick. The interest of the building resides in its exterior and its setting.

◆

CROUCH END
Hornsey Town Hall c1965
In the early 1930s an architectural competition was won by a young New Zealand architect, R H Uren, for a new town hall in the Broadway, with a design very closely allied to Dudok's Town Hall at Hilversum. The superb building, enhanced by attention to detail both outside and inside, stands proud behind a somewhat bland grassed forecourt. To the right of the photograph, and clearly visible, are A J Ayres' fine stone relief panels, a tribute to the gas industry, on a lesser building by Uren.

CROUCH END, CHRIST CHURCH, CROUCH END HILL c1965 C582009

CROUCH END, HORNSEY TOWN HALL c1965 C582011

CROUCH END, HORNSEY TOWN HALL FORECOURT c1965 C582010

CROUCH END
Hornsey Town Hall Forecourt c1965
A minimal circular fountain typical of the 1930s is Uren's only gesture to forecourt landscaping. The area has tended to be a problem for the council, as there is a strong temptation to create a car park in front of the Town Hall, but praise be, at the moment it remains grassed and treed.

◆

EASTCOTE
Field End Road c1965
Eastcote is a mediaeval settlement; it is only as one emerges from the shopping parades of the 1930s grouped around the underground station into a series of timber-framed vernacular buildings of the 16th century, that one realises that the original village centre was well to the north of the present one. Among the old buildings, close to the new centre, is Barn House, an early barn conversion of little merit, Field End Farm House, Field End Lodge and Retreat Cottage, all timber-framed.

EASTCOTE, FIELD END ROAD c1965 E178001

EASTCOTE, FIELD END ROAD 1965 E178002

The builder T F Nash was one of three main contributors to the creation of the present shopping centre. The almost Arts and Crafts Deane Parade on the far right of the photograph is typical of his pleasant but unexciting buildings. Note that the road through Eastcote is exceptionally wide for a small suburban centre.

EASTCOTE, THE CASE IS ALTERED, HIGH ROAD 1965 E178006

In 1891 a fire caused considerable damage to the fabric of the building, and the impression from the photograph is of a complete rebuilding soon after that date. From an internal inspection, however, it is soon clear that the 17th century was not completely obliterated in its dark friendly bar. To the left of the photograph a glimpse is afforded of a weather-boarded timber barn converted relatively recently to restaurant use. It is a pity that the setting of the building has not entirely retained its rural air.

EAST FINCHLEY, HIGH ROAD LOOKING SOUTH c1965 E199012

To the south-east of mediaeval Finchley, the High Road drops down from the North Circular Road between an almost standard series of parade shops built around the turn of the century, and past the Rex Cinema built in 1910, among the earliest in Greater London. At the foot of the hill is the brick and concrete underground station of 1939, designed by Charles Holden and L H Bucknell. On a building excelling in proportion rather than decoration, the prominent statue of an archer by E Aumonier provides relief.

EDGWARE, THE BY-PASS, MOAT MOUNT c1960 E126046

The A1 sweeps north between Moat Mound Recreation Ground and Mill Hill Golf Club, and is little changed since it was built, apart from the introduction of high level lighting standards. At the turn of the millennium we long for those halcyon days as traffic now reaches saturation point, potholes get deeper and deeper, and road repairs are always carried out at the most inconvenient spot on the road, invariably with scant evidence of work in action!

ENFIELD,
THE TOWN AND CHURCH STREET
c1965 E179041
Once tree-lined, the pavement edge to
the right of the photograph has given
itself up to signage and lighting
standards. The drinking fountain with
its cherub ornament was erected in
1884; Barclay's Bank on the right was
designed by Gilbert Scott, and dates
from 1897. On the site of Pearsons
until the mid 1920s was Enfield Palace,
which probably gained its name as the
inheritor of parts of the demolished
Elsyng Palace to the north of the town,
which lay within the Forty Hall estate.

ENFIELD

The Market Place c1965 E179038

The timber market cross dominates the photograph; to its left is
the King's Head with its tile hanging and timbering, a finely-
detailed town pub of 1899 by Shoebridge and Rising. These
architects specialised in pub design, and quality shines through;
similar quality can be seen at The Crown, an exuberant pub in
Cricklewood Broadway, and The Rising Sun in Chalton Street,
Euston. To its right is the beautiful mediaeval parish church of St
Andrew in its leafy churchyard, exhibiting features attributable to
every period since the 12th century. It has been 'restored' more
than once, but it is often open and a must for the town visitor.
Having perambulated the town centre, much more is to be enjoyed
in the walks to the north of the church.

ENFIELD, GENTLEMANS ROW c1965 E179046
To the west of the town centre, and parallel with Chase side, this picturesque street has to be seen by any visitor to Enfield. Its buildings range in date from late mediaeval timber frames to early 19th-century flat-fronted brick houses, some at its northern end opening onto the River Lea. Also at the northern end, for the thirsty, is the Crown and Horseshoes Pub, which is attractively situated on the river.

FINCHLEY, THE GOLF COURSE, GORDON ROAD c1965 F64031
The nineteenth hole is to be found in Nether Court, a free-standing neo-Jacobean mansion by Percy Stone. The course, one of many within Greater London, occupies a stretch of land extending south from Frith Manor to the Dollis Brook. Although suburbia laps around its southern edges, the course does, in part, retain a well-treed, almost rural atmosphere.

FINCHLEY, BALLARDS LANE c1965 F64055
Ballards Lane is a straight, uninteresting road which effectively forms a link between Finchley Road and Tally Ho Corner.
The Edwardian buildings in the photograph have changed little, apart from losing their rather elegant shop fronts.

FINCHLEY, HIGH ROAD c1965 F64071
This somewhat featureless shopping centre has developed to the north of the Tally Ho pub and Tally Ho corner,
which can be seen as a multi-gabled vista stopper in this photograph. Vague echoes of C F A Voysey are to be seen in
the higher building in the centre; the demolition of W E Trent's Gaumont Cinema to the south of the Tally Ho in
the late 1980s was a loss to the area as a whole.

FRIERN BARNET
Halliwick Hospital, Friern Barnet Road c1965 F187014
This functional machine for healing people, quite new when the
photograph was taken, contrasts dramatically in its simple, almost
domestic design with its very close neighbour, the Colney Hatch
Asylum to its south-east. Here is a pauper asylum of gigantic
proportions, built to house 1,000 patients and designed by S W
Daukes in 1851. As with Hanwell Asylum, the humanitarian
principles evolving from revised scientific thinking were
implemented, but even so, the long, cold corridors were seriously
intimidating. Much of this remarkable building has been
demolished over the past decade to accommodate a not
particularly complimentary flat conversion.

◆

FRIERN BARNET, ST JAMES'S CHURCH, FRIERN BARNET LANE c1965 F187018
In the 12th century Friern Barnet belonged to the Hospital of St John of Jerusalem, and the church, notwithstanding extensive mid 19th-century additions, dates from around that time. Picturesque in its remarkably rural surroundings, its building materials include examples of a geological oddity: blocks of iron cemented gravel-stone (Fericrete), which is also to be seen in the base of Manor Farm barn, Harmondsworth and in St Mary's Church, Bedfont, close to Heathrow.

GOLDERS GREEN, GOLDERS GREEN ROAD c1965 G271009
Golders Green was farmland until the turn of the century; prosperity came in 1905 with the arrival of the Northern line. It is famous for its crematorium, partly designed by Sir Ernest George. The London Crematorium Company had anticipated a population explosion and bought its land cheaply in 1902. The photograph looks between earlier development on the right, dated 1909, and the more prominent buildings of 1913 by H A Welsh. In the distance is the town centre church of St Alban and St Michael, 1933, by Sir Giles Gilbert Scott, a pleasing design with its lantern tower and simple Gothic detailing.

GOLDERS GREEN, THE WAR MEMORIAL AND GOLDERS GREEN ROAD c1965 G271012

An Edwardian, steeply-gabled terrace of shops and flats overlooks the dignified stone island War Memorial of 1923, with its stepped approach. This well-ordered scene is typical of the high quality ambience of the suburb as a whole, and well anticipated by the Midland Bank with its impressive, yet restrained, neo-classical frontage, exactly as a bank should be.

GOLDERS GREEN, THE BUS STATION, NORTH END ROAD c1960 G271038

The least attractive part of the town centre is the forecourt to the underground station, which is also used as a bus station. Rather than admire this tarmac desert, it is better to turn through 180° to see, and if possible visit, the Golders Green Hippodrome, designed by Bertie Crew in 1913. This fine theatre has been used by the BBC as a recording studio since the late 1960s; it is one of comparatively few remaining suburban music halls in Greater London outside the West End.

HARROW, COMMERCIAL DEVELOPMENT, VICTORIA ROAD c1965 S642006

After the Second World War, it took a decade and more for the economy to recover, but by the end of the 1950s buildings of this type were beginning to burgeon almost anywhere. This represented the brave new architectural world of big must be good, especially so far as the developer, the builder and the architect were concerned. Speculative building, with its possibility of great rewards, was the order of the day. Some of these monsters are now considered by students of the 1950s and 1960s to be of historic interest, but this proposition is very difficult to support.

HARROW, STATION ROAD c1960 H429035

Timber gables and full-height faceted bay windows create an imposing range of shops and flats of the early 20th century. It is unfortunate that the impact of the design has been diluted by the use of oversized shop fascias, especially to Bennetts. The neo-Georgian North Thames Gas Board showroom is a bland intrusion.

HARROW-ON-THE-HILL
High Street c1965 H27115

A Saxon hill village, known as Gumeninga Hergae, or the shrine of Guma's people, in 767, it has now become well and truly subsumed into suburbia, and into Betjeman folklore through his poem of the same name written around 1954. The presence of the school, which was founded by a local farmer, John Lyon, in 1572, has brought fame, but at the same time has undoubtedly contributed to the present fossilisation of the village as a self-supporting commercial centre. The High Street is without doubt extremely attractive, and the school buildings contribute greatly to that well-manicured ambience, such as Bradbys to the left and The Park seen here to the right, a fine house remodelled by John Nash of Regent Street fame, with landscaped gardens by Capability Brown.

◆

HARROW-ON-THE-HILL, HIGH STREET c1960
This view looks across to St Mary's parish church. The High Street, with its attractive mix of buildings, does conceal some of its many charms. The buildings to the immediate left house the remains of a range of timber-framed cottages; their end frame has been exposed to view within the former building contractor's offices. Externally in forty years the view has hardly changed at all.

HARROW-ON-THE-HILL, HIGH STREET AND CHURCH HILL c1965 H27144
Sixty years and two world wars on from the photograph of 1906, the late 18th-century house on Church Hill has been demolished and replaced by the War Memorial Building, designed by Sir Herbert Baker in 1921, built in remembrance of almost 700 old Harrovians who fell in the First World War. Their names are recorded in the Golden Book, housed within the building. Fronting Old School and the War Memorial Building is an attractive series of balustrades and steps by Sir Edwin Lutyens of the 1930s. On the extreme left is Druries by C F Hayward, a building said to be a favourite of John Betjeman.

HARROW-ON-THE-HILL, THE SPEECH ROOM, GROVE HILL c1960 H429022
From The Grove the camera looks south to a view dominated by William Burges's Speech Room with its polychrome brickwork; the tower, by the local architect Charles Nicholson, was not added until 1919. Close to the camera is the Art Schools of 1891 by W C Marshall, which is not of particular merit, but the stone medallions of Reynolds and Hogarth added in 1919 are quite fine.

HATCH END, THE BROADWAY c1965 H404021
The placename is derived from Haecc or gate. The village is on the north-west edge of Pinner Park, itself a 14th-century deer park owned by the Archbishop of Canterbury. Although not designated an Ancient Monument, it is with its extensive boundary banks the best example of its type in Middlesex. Hatch End has expanded since the arrival of the railway in the mid 1840s, but The Broadway is of little architectural interest. However, of considerable interest is St Anselms Church, Westfield Park, with its superb Arts and Crafts glass by Louis Davis.

HENDON, THE TOWN HALL, THE BURROUGHS c1965 H397125

Walk away from Watford Way to the east along The Burroughs towards the original village centre. There are 18th- and 19th-century houses, and a fine group of public buildings comprising the Town Hall of 1900, the Public Library of 1929, the Fire Station of 1911 and, at the junction with Church End, the 13th-century church of St Mary should be seen, as should the museum housed in Church Farm House close by. By now you may be quite tired, so adjourn to the Greyhound Inn or The Chequers for a re-invigorating drink.

HENDON, THE BROADWAY c1965 H397147

This photograph highlights one of the joys of suburban development: the changes in date, scale and design of buildings within a comparatively short distance of one another. The house of around 1870 in the foreground, with its added bungalow shop front, the decorative terrace of the 1880s and the later gabled residential turn-of-the-century buildings, while not individually special, are collectively attractive, and each a piece in London's great jigsaw.

KENTON, KENTON ROAD LOOKING EAST c1960 K151012

Looking at this view, it is difficult to envisage the hamlet of Keninton mentioned in the Feet of Fines in 1232. All is of the 30s, including the row of sub-Arts and Crafts shops, and on the right the small buildings originally associated with the railway. In the distance can be seen the loosely-interpreted Gothic church of St Mary, 1936, by J Harold Gibbons, an architect whose reputation is growing steadily.

KINGSBURY, HOLY INNOCENTS PARISH CHURCH, KINGSBURY ROAD c1965 K142040

William Butterfield is one of the masters of late 19th-century architecture, but here is a slight hiccup in his portfolio of outstanding works. Designed in 1884, the stock brick building, with its peculiar octagonal west turret, cannot be said to be of particular interest either inside or outside.

KINGSBURY
St Andrew's Old Church, Church Lane c1960 K142001

Except in this enclave, it is difficult to imagine that Kingsbury did not originate in the 1930s as part of the engulfing suburban sea. It is, however, the Chingesberie mentioned in Domesday, and the Kynges byrig in the Index to the Charters and Rolls of 1046. The Old Church, a small picturesque building of at least the 12th century, nestles in its tombstoned, grassy churchyard, a churchyard it shares with St Andrews Church. It is sad that respect for this venerable church is scant around Kingsbury, where it has suffered considerably from vandalism over the years. Both the grade one church and its churchyard are included in English Heritage's Register of Buildings at Risk in Greater London.

KINGSBURY
St Andrew's Church, Church Lane c1965

In contrast to the picturesque qualities of St Andrews Old Church to its south, the late arrival has a not surprisingly metropolitan arrogance, as it was moved stone by stone from Well Street, close to Oxford Circus, in 1934. Externally not unattractive, it is the interior which is of considerable moment: the reredos, chancel screen and pulpit were designed by George Edmund Street, the sedilia by John Loughborough Pearson, the lectern by William Butterfield and the stained glass by Clayton and Bell. This is not an area much frequented by tourists, but the two churches are well worthy of a detour.

◆

KINGSBURY
The Prince of Wales Pub c1960

As the suburban semi-detached house with its timbering and Tudor detailing reflected the Englishman's home as his castle, so with the contemporary pubs. Similar to others in almost every suburb, the Prince of Wales continues the theme, offering safe and comfortable drinking to new suburban man; a competently-designed exterior opens into a timbered bar with matching fittings and furniture. It is regrettable that the large brewery chains have generally done away with both the fittings and the furniture in order to create the new family pub of the 21st century.

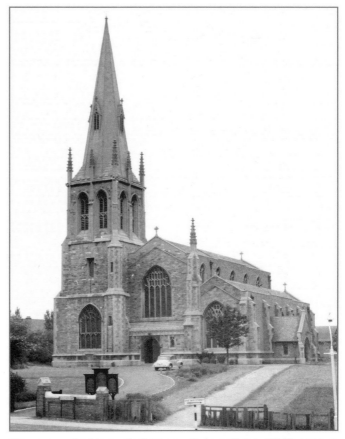

KINGSBURY, ST ANDREW'S CHURCH, CHURCH LANE c1965 K142043

KINGSBURY, THE PRINCE OF WALES PUB c1960 K142014

KINGSBURY,
KINGSBURY ROAD c1965
K142022

Kingsbury Underground Station is situated some distance to the north-west of the original village centre, and within a range of not unattractive shops, seen on the right, with their pitched dormered and tiled roofs and tall chimneys. The Gaumont Cinema on the opposite side of the road offers an almost brutalist contrasting elevation. It is difficult to believe, looking at Kingsbury Road, that the area retains many field hedges and trees; they were preserved quite carefully in the laying out of the 1930s estates, a definite plus for the local council of the day.

**KINGSBURY,
KINGSBURY ROAD c1960**
K142028
This busy shopping street has
buildings of human scale of the 1920s
and 30s, with a prominent
well-designed Midland Bank sign now
replaced by the anonymous HSBC
of the Eastern Banking Empire.

MILL HILL, WATFORD WAY c1960 M357018
Watford Way, running down to the North Circular Road from the M1 motorway, looks definitely under-used in 1960. It would have been pleasant enough to live alongside a relatively up-market road of wide verges and young trees, illuminated by attractive street lighting. Today traffic streams in all directions, and residents sit looking out from behind noise-reducing double-glazed windows.

MILL HILL, THE BROADWAY c1965 M357049
Here we see an attractive group of sub-Arts and Crafts buildings with steeply-pitched roofs and tile-hung dormer windows over an open timber balcony. The shop front of W H Smith & Son is well-designed, and Barclay's Bank used a reticent, yet confident, typescript on their fascias. A precursor to the deterioration in town and village centre design is to be seen in the refenestration of the first floor to W H Smiths.

MILL HILL, THE VILLAGE POND, THE RIDGEWAY c1965 M357058

This lovely village extends from Highwood Hill to the north to Mill Hill East underground station in the south. This view across the pond towards the rather miserable brick church is standard artist's stuff, but the buildings, including Mill Hill School, some of 1825, Belmont of 1773, by James Paine junior, the Missionary Institute of 1778 by John Johnson, who designed Leicester's County Rooms, along with any smaller buildings, should be seen by wandering at leisure from the underground station northwards to the attractive Rising Sun pub, and on again via Totteridge village to High Barnet underground station, a distance of about five miles.

NORTH HARROW, PINNER ROAD c1965 N177016

This featureless wave of suburbia grew up in the 1930s to cover the fields between Harrow-on-the-Hill and Pinner. It includes shops to cater for semi-detached commuters into the City, a church and offices. At the divide, under the clock tower, the left-hand fork heads for Pinner village, while the right-hand one will cut through the mediaeval deer park at Pinner Park to Hatch End.

NORTH HARROW
Headstone Manor c1965 N177009

The camera looks at the early 16th-century Great Barn, which was originally one of four opening onto the farmyard; a second smaller one has quite recently been particularly well restored from a skeletal state following a fire in 1979. The scene has changed radically from this shrub-laden view of 1965; the Barn was converted to museum/community use in 1973, and sin of sins, was reclad using waney-edged elm boarding! Headstone Manor itself is sited within a square moat to the east of the barn, and dates from the mid 14th century. It is without doubt one of the most important timber-framed halls in Greater London. It is in the ownership of the local council, but instead of being open to view, it has resided under a quite spectacular plastic cover for some years awaiting sympathetic repair and restoration. One day it will happen, but it will have been a very long wait.

OAKWOOD, THE UNDERGROUND STATION, BRAMLEY ROAD c1965 O105004

One stop short of the terminus at Cockfosters, Oakwood Station is one of the jewels along this northern stretch of the Piccadilly line, which also includes Southgate, Arnos Grove and Cockfosters. Working on a theme echoed at Northfields and Sudbury Town, Charles Holden designed these brick and concrete stations soon after 1933 with a flair and panache surpassed by no other designer on the system.

OAKWOOD, BRAMLEY ROAD c1965 O105023

Looking west, the camera captures the underground station in its rather austere setting. The neighbouring shops, built around the time of the station, with their Crittall windows and regular fronts, hidden just to the left of the camera, set a similar austere tone. It is Trent Park extending away to the left that provides a welcome relief and contrast.

OAKWOOD, BRAMLEY ROAD c1965 O105015

With the arrival of the Piccadilly Line came an influx of commuters, and with this influx came the promise of commercial profits. Thus, close to Oakwood Station this parade of typical 1930s small shops was built. The retention of the trees softening their setting is to be welcomed - but for how long, when in most parts of London insurance companies break out in a cold sweat at the very sight of a suburban tree. Look around and see the so-called 'pruning' carried out by nervous councils as they virtually destroy a superb visual asset.

OAKWOOD, THE PARK c1965 O105011

This pavilion obviously caught the photographer's eye as an oddity; it probably would today as well, with its strange mansard-type roof, timbered gables and waney-edged boarding. Being so peculiar, it does not jar overmuch in its obviously much earlier parkland setting.

OAKWOOD, ST THOMAS'S CHURCH, PRINCE GEORGE AVENUE c1965 O105019
Literally just around the corner from the underground station is St Thomas's Church, designed by Romilly and Craze in an unspectacular suburban style in 1941, to serve the newly-arrived local community. The treeless frontage fails to raise any spiritual hope here, even with the spikey steeple added in 1965.

PALMERS GREEN, BROOMFIELD PARK, BROOMFIELD LANE c1965 P295018
Municipalised now, this reduced park was, in the 16th century, owned by Geoffrey Walkaden, but by 1625 it had passed to Joseph Jackson, a merchant, in whose family it remained until it was removed by marriage. In the early 1800s it passed to the Powys family, and was finally bought by Southgate Council in 1903. As well as the usual statutory facilities, such as tennis courts and a football ground, there is an attractive series of lakes and ponds, as well as Broomfield House with its stableyard, an early 18th-century summer house and a Garden of Remembrance opened in 1929.

PALMERS GREEN, BROOMFIELD HOUSE, BROOMFIELD LANE c1965 P295020

Broomfield House has a complicated history. It expanded around a simple timber-framed late mediaeval building. Through the 16th century, and into the 17th, rooms were added; in c1820 the brick wing clearly visible in the photograph was built. The fake timbering was a slightly ridiculous whim of the Borough Council in 1928. By far the most important asset of the house was the grand staircase of c1720, with its decorative mural by Gerard Lanscroon of 1726. A structural analysis of the house was undertaken by Richard Lea of English Heritage in 1994.

PALMERS GREEN, BROOMFIELD HOUSE, BROOMFIELD LANE c1965 P295013

The London Borough of Enfield will not be remembered for its sympathetic approach to the conservation of its historic buildings. Whilst in its care, the building has been a museum and a café, among other things, but owing to a series of fires in 1984, 1993 and 1994 it has been reduced to a sad remnant. Only by the grace of God were the Lanscroon paintings rescued. At the time of writing no certain use has been found for this inevitably deteriorating building, which is of considerable architectural importance.

PALMERS GREEN, BROOMFIELD HOUSE, BROOMFIELD LANE c1965 P295002
The tulips bloom in beautiful profusion, and the house is reflected in the almost glassy stillness of the pond. Today the gardens are included in the English Heritage Register of Parks and Gardens of Special Historic Interest; and yet here in the heart of affluent suburbia, the condition of this major house is described by English Heritage as very bad and of the adjacent stables as poor. Enough said.

PALMERS GREEN, THE TRIANGLE, GREEN LANES c1965 P295007
The buildings here reflect the early 20th-century origins of Palmers Green; the triangle is all that remains of the original green. The A1004 swings right into Alderman's Hill past the railway station, and the outstanding building facing the camera is of 1904. On the right the anthemion-dominated free Classical building, by Evans and Davies, and the roughcast upper stories to Hamells, provide a very acceptable streetscape.

PALMERS GREEN, GREEN LANES c1965 P295009

Well-mannered town centre buildings open onto the flower-bedecked triangle, but the portents of a more gaudy future are already apparent. Look at the ABC Restaurant with its oversized advertising, and Foodtown's inappropriate lettering and enlarged fascia. Look further down Green Lanes, and see the familiar dreary three-storey legacy of the late 1950s stopping the view.

PINNER, HIGH STREET c1965 P296029

The scene has changed very little since 1955, except that this fine street has been blighted by the thoughtless introduction of ugly lighting columns; the parking problems, very apparent in 2000, are beginning to emerge. Approached by a discreet mall, there is now a supermarket situated behind the buildings on the left.

PINNER, HIGH STREET c1965 P296030

A striking building in the High Street is The Queen's Head Pub, mainly of the 17th century, with its welcoming atmospheric bars. At the centre, secreted away within an 18th-century brick skin, is a superb late mediaeval hall house, complete with a fine crown post roof and an original window on the rear elevation. The attractive single-storey building at the end of the street (Lewis and Day) has been demolished.

RUISLIP, BURY STREET LOOKING SOUTH c1965 R335047

There is perhaps a brighter face to the village centre today than is apparent in the photograph, although the traffic problem is ghastly. St Martins Church still dominates the centre, a particularly fine building with an atmosphere of truly rural godliness as opposed to its being a spiritual centre of metroland. In architectural terms it has much to offer within its basically 13th-century fabric: a 17th-century bread cupboard, hatchments, wall paintings and monuments, including one to Jane Clitherow who died in 1659, probably by Joshua Marshall. For further reading see 'The Goodliest Place In Middlesex' by Eileen M Boult, published in 1989 by Hillingdon Borough Libraries.

RUISLIP, HIGH STREET c1965 R335051

RUISLIP
High Street c1965

The camera looks away from the original village centre into the alternative Ruislip of the 1930s and towards the Metropolitan line station of 1904. It is an attractive, almost domestic building, now somewhat blighted by modern office development. On the south side of the station is the Barn Hotel, an attractive timber-framed complex incorporating a very tipsy barn.

RUISLIP
The Lido, Reservoir Road c1965

The Lido is situated about a mile to the north of Ruislip village. The grounds were laid out by T H Mawson in 1936, during the era of outdoor pool building, and in this context the Lido is special on account of its grand scale. The main building, designed by G W Smith, has now been converted reasonably sympathetically into a pub, and the miniature railway which skirted the water's edge on the opposite bank remains as something of a reminder of those balmy pre-war days.

RUISLIP, THE LIDO, RESERVOIR ROAD c1965 R335077

SOUTHGATE, CHASE SIDE c1965 S641060

Taking its name from the south gate to Enfield Chase, and overlooking the Lea Valley, Southgate was a part of Edmonton until the late 19th century. Development began in around 1870 with the arrival of the Great Northern Railway, but it was the arrival of the Piccadilly Line in 1933 that produced mass housing. Although the original village green is away to the south, along the High Street it is the superbly spacious circular underground station by Charles Holden, and the grassy roundabout, that create a new focus of interest.

SOUTH HARROW, NORTHOLT ROAD LOOKING NORTH c1965 S642019

Archetypal 1930s development swishes around the foot of Harrow on the Hill, with its gasworks tower always visible from the village and on the approach to Northolt Aerodrome. The cars in the photograph are of more interest than the buildings.

STANMORE
Old Church, Uxbridge Road c1965 S180070

The picturesque growth of trees and ivy which has been allowed to
flourish unchecked took its toll on the brick structure, and the
church, probably designed by Nicholas Stone and consecrated by
Archbishop Laud in 1632, has had to be defoliated and properly
consolidated in recent years. The graveyard, with its good
collection of 18th-century tombs, has also been cleared and mown.
At the time of writing, this remarkable building is visually
threatened by a proposal to build an estate of run-of-the-mill
houses and flats on the redundant RAF Stanmore, immediately to
the west of the churchyard boundary.

STANMORE, THE BROADWAY c1965 S180073

This interesting photograph should ideally be read with that taken from almost the same spot in 1906. On the left are the shops which came with the 1930s transformation of this previously rural area, while on the right is the Ernest Bernays Memorial Institute of 1870, only really attractive when compared with the buildings opposite! Further along The Broadway, and set back, is a row of shops which in fact incorporate a fragment of The Red House. This row was demolished in the 1980s to make space for a large office block. In the distance can be seen the jettied row of cottages, now offices, which identify the 1906 photograph.

WEMBLEY PARK, OLYMPIC WAY (CUP FINAL DAY c1960) W314029

The twin towers have been an inspiring sporting symbol since the stadium was built in 1923 as part of the British Empire Exhibition. The approach from Wembley Park underground station, romantically named Olympic Way, has changed little in the years since the 1948 London Olympic Games, but in recent years the setting of the stadium from this viewpoint has been quite drastically remodelled. Was the money well spent? Well, maybe not, if the multi-million pound National Stadium rebuilding programme materialises within the foreseeable future.

WEMBLEY PARK, THE STADIUM c1965 W314019

Built on the site of a failed attempt to erect a structure to rival the Eiffel Tower, this building, apart from its twin pepper-pot towers, cannot be said to be a thing of great beauty. Along with most other exhibition buildings, the stadium is constructed in ferro-concrete, and for the most part the structures were expected to be demolished after the six-month planned exhibition run. A few remain; these include the Palace of Industry and fragments of the Palace of Arts, where concrete decay has revealed that reinforcement extended to handfuls of nails thrown into the mix. A notable addition on the site is, of course, the superb Wembley Arena, designed by Sir Owen Williams in 1934.

WEMBLEY PARK, WEMBLEY PARK DRIVE c1960 W314069

A contrast to the stadium complex, and the numerous large office blocks that have materialised over the past twenty years, particularly along Empire Way, the road swings to rise up to the Wembley Park Underground Station of 1923. The attractive domestic-scale shops look even better when compared to the intrusive, faceless Columbus Dixon office block.

WEMBLEY PARK
Barn Hill c1965

A mile to the north of the stadium, Barn Hill takes about itself an air of rural contemplation as the camera looks out to the surrounding hills. What better on a summer's day than to unpack a picnic, set up the deckchairs, be attacked by wasps and eaten by insects!

WEMBLEY PARK
Barn Hill c1965

This is a children's paradise: blend open grass, trees and a pond with a lively imagination, and a never-ending variety of worlds can be created in a single afternoon - and lost forever in later years.

WEMBLEY PARK, BARN HILL 1965 W576130

WEMBLEY PARK, BARN HILL 1965 W576132

WOOD GREEN
Alexandra Palace c1965 W626012

The Palace was built to rival the Crystal Palace on Sydenham Hill in South London. A former International Exhibition Hall, and a 'Peoples Palace', the first building was designed by John Johnson and Alfred Meeson, and opened in 1873. Sixteen days later it was burnt down, and was rebuilt by John Johnson to re-open in 1875. It was never a great success; part was leased to the BBC in 1934, and television broadcasts began in 1936. In 1966 the Greater London Council took over the building, and in 1980 it passed on to Haringey Borough Council. Following yet another serious fire, the Palace was restored in 1980-88 by the Alexandra Palace Development Team. Although much of the building is now in regular use, the integral theatre remains desperately in need of restoration.

◆

Index

Frith Book Co Titles

www.francisfrith.co.uk

The Frith Book Company publishes over 100 new titles each year. A selection of those currently available are listed below. For latest catalogue please contact Frith Book Co.

Town Books 96 pages, approx 100 photos. County and Themed Books 128 pages, approx 150 photos (unless specified). All titles hardback laminated case and jacket except those indicated pb (paperback)

Amersham, Chesham & Rickmansworth (pb)		
	1-85937-340-2	£9.99
Ancient Monuments & Stone Circles	1-85937-143-4	£17.99
Aylesbury (pb)	1-85937-227-9	£9.99
Bakewell	1-85937-113-2	£12.99
Barnstaple (pb)	1-85937-300-3	£9.99
Bath (pb)	1-85937-419-0	£9.99
Bedford (pb)	1-85937-205-8	£9.99
Berkshire (pb)	1-85937-191-4	£9.99
Berkshire Churches	1-85937-170-1	£17.99
Blackpool (pb)	1-85937-382-8	£9.99
Bognor Regis (pb)	1-85937-431-x	£9.99
Bournemouth	1-85937-067-5	£12.99
Bradford (pb)	1-85937-204-x	£9.99
Brighton & Hove(pb)	1-85937-192-2	£8.99
Bristol (pb)	1-85937-264-3	£9.99
British Life A Century Ago (pb)	1-85937-213-9	£9.99
Buckinghamshire (pb)	1-85937-200-7	£9.99
Camberley (pb)	1-85937-222-8	£9.99
Cambridge (pb)	1-85937-422-0	£9.99
Cambridgeshire (pb)	1-85937-420-4	£9.99
Canals & Waterways (pb)	1-85937-291-0	£9.99
Canterbury Cathedral (pb)	1-85937-179-5	£9.99
Cardiff (pb)	1-85937-093-4	£9.99
Carmarthenshire	1-85937-216-3	£14.99
Chelmsford (pb)	1-85937-310-0	£9.99
Cheltenham (pb)	1-85937-095-0	£9.99
Cheshire (pb)	1-85937-271-6	£9.99
Chester	1-85937-090-x	£12.99
Chesterfield	1-85937-378-x	£9.99
Chichester (pb)	1-85937-228-7	£9.99
Colchester (pb)	1-85937-188-4	£8.99
Cornish Coast	1-85937-163-9	£14.99
Cornwall (pb)	1-85937-229-5	£9.99
Cornwall Living Memories	1-85937-248-1	£14.99
Cotswolds (pb)	1-85937-230-9	£9.99
Cotswolds Living Memories	1-85937-255-4	£14.99
County Durham	1-85937-123-x	£14.99
Croydon Living Memories	1-85937-162-0	£9.99
Cumbria	1-85937-101-9	£14.99
Dartmoor	1-85937-145-0	£14.99
Derby (pb)	1-85937-367-4	£9.99
Derbyshire (pb)	1-85937-196-5	£9.99
Devon (pb)	1-85937-297-x	£9.99
Dorset (pb)	1-85937-269-4	£9.99
Dorset Churches	1-85937-172-8	£17.99
Dorset Coast (pb)	1-85937-299-6	£9.99
Dorset Living Memories	1-85937-210-4	£14.99
Down the Severn	1-85937-118-3	£14.99
Down the Thames (pb)	1-85937-278-3	£9.99
Down the Trent	1-85937-311-9	£14.99
Dublin (pb)	1-85937-231-7	£9.99
East Anglia (pb)	1-85937-265-1	£9.99
East London	1-85937-080-2	£14.99
East Sussex	1-85937-130-2	£14.99
Eastbourne	1-85937-061-6	£12.99
Edinburgh (pb)	1-85937-193-0	£8.99
England in the 1880s	1-85937-331-3	£17.99
English Castles (pb)	1-85937-434-4	£9.99
English Country Houses	1-85937-161-2	£17.99
Essex (pb)	1-85937-270-8	£9.99
Exeter	1-85937-126-4	£12.99
Exmoor	1-85937-132-9	£14.99
Falmouth	1-85937-066-7	£12.99
Folkestone (pb)	1-85937-124-8	£9.99
Glasgow (pb)	1-85937-190-6	£9.99
Gloucestershire	1-85937-102-7	£14.99
Great Yarmouth (pb)	1-85937-426-3	£9.99
Greater Manchester (pb)	1-85937-266-x	£9.99
Guildford (pb)	1-85937-410-7	£9.99
Hampshire (pb)	1-85937-279-1	£9.99
Hampshire Churches (pb)	1-85937-207-4	£9.99
Harrogate	1-85937-423-9	£9.99
Hastings & Bexhill (pb)	1-85937-131-0	£9.99
Heart of Lancashire (pb)	1-85937-197-3	£9.99
Helston (pb)	1-85937-214-7	£9.99
Hereford (pb)	1-85937-175-2	£9.99
Herefordshire	1-85937-174-4	£14.99
Hertfordshire (pb)	1-85937-247-3	£9.99
Horsham (pb)	1-85937-432-8	£9.99
Humberside	1-85937-215-5	£14.99
Hythe, Romney Marsh & Ashford	1-85937-256-2	£9.99

Available from your local bookshop or from the publisher

Frith Book Co Titles (continued)

Ipswich (pb)	1-85937-424-7	£9.99	St Ives (pb)	1-85937415-8	£9.99
Ireland (pb)	1-85937-181-7	£9.99	Scotland (pb)	1-85937-182-5	£9.99
Isle of Man (pb)	1-85937-268-6	£9.99	Scottish Castles (pb)	1-85937-323-2	£9.99
Isles of Scilly	1-85937-136-1	£14.99	Sevenoaks & Tunbridge	1-85937-057-8	£12.99
Isle of Wight (pb)	1-85937-429-8	£9.99	Sheffield, South Yorks (pb)	1-85937-267-8	£9.99
Isle of Wight Living Memories	1-85937-304-6	£14.99	Shrewsbury (pb)	1-85937-325-9	£9.99
Kent (pb)	1-85937-189-2	£9.99	Shropshire (pb)	1-85937-326-7	£9.99
Kent Living Memories	1-85937-125-6	£14.99	Somerset	1-85937-153-1	£14.99
Lake District (pb)	1-85937-275-9	£9.99	South Devon Coast	1-85937-107-8	£14.99
Lancaster, Morecambe & Heysham (pb)	1-85937-233-3	£9.99	South Devon Living Memories	1-85937-168-x	£14.99
Leeds (pb)	1-85937-202-3	£9.99	South Hams	1-85937-220-1	£14.99
Leicester	1-85937-073-x	£12.99	Southampton (pb)	1-85937-427-1	£9.99
Leicestershire (pb)	1-85937-185-x	£9.99	Southport (pb)	1-85937-425-5	£9.99
Lincolnshire (pb)	1-85937-433-6	£9.99	Staffordshire	1-85937-047-0	£12.99
Liverpool & Merseyside (pb)	1-85937-234-1	£9.99	Stratford upon Avon	1-85937-098-5	£12.99
London (pb)	1-85937-183-3	£9.99	Suffolk (pb)	1-85937-221-x	£9.99
Ludlow (pb)	1-85937-176-0	£9.99	Suffolk Coast	1-85937-259-7	£14.99
Luton (pb)	1-85937-235-x	£9.99	Surrey (pb)	1-85937-240-6	£9.99
Maidstone	1-85937-056-x	£14.99	Sussex (pb)	1-85937-184-1	£9.99
Manchester (pb)	1-85937-198-1	£9.99	Swansea (pb)	1-85937-167-1	£9.99
Middlesex	1-85937-158-2	£14.99	Tees Valley & Cleveland	1-85937-211-2	£14.99
New Forest	1-85937-128-0	£14.99	Thanet (pb)	1-85937-116-7	£9.99
Newark (pb)	1-85937-366-6	£9.99	Tiverton (pb)	1-85937-178-7	£9.99
Newport, Wales (pb)	1-85937-258-9	£9.99	Torbay	1-85937-063-2	£12.99
Newquay (pb)	1-85937-421-2	£9.99	Truro	1-85937-147-7	£12.99
Norfolk (pb)	1-85937-195-7	£9.99	Victorian and Edwardian Cornwall	1-85937-252-x	£14.99
Norfolk Living Memories	1-85937-217-1	£14.99	Victorian & Edwardian Devon	1-85937-253-8	£14.99
Northamptonshire	1-85937-150-7	£14.99	Victorian & Edwardian Kent	1-85937-149-3	£14.99
Northumberland Tyne & Wear (pb)	1-85937-281-3	£9.99	Vic & Ed Maritime Album	1-85937-144-2	£17.99
North Devon Coast	1-85937-146-9	£14.99	Victorian and Edwardian Sussex	1-85937-157-4	£14.99
North Devon Living Memories	1-85937-261-9	£14.99	Victorian & Edwardian Yorkshire	1-85937-154-x	£14.99
North London	1-85937-206-6	£14.99	Victorian Seaside	1-85937-159-0	£17.99
North Wales (pb)	1-85937-298-8	£9.99	Villages of Devon (pb)	1-85937-293-7	£9.99
North Yorkshire (pb)	1-85937-236-8	£9.99	Villages of Kent (pb)	1-85937-294-5	£9.99
Norwich (pb)	1-85937-194-9	£8.99	Villages of Sussex (pb)	1-85937-295-3	£9.99
Nottingham (pb)	1-85937-324-0	£9.99	Warwickshire (pb)	1-85937-203-1	£9.99
Nottinghamshire (pb)	1-85937-187-6	£9.99	Welsh Castles (pb)	1-85937-322-4	£9.99
Oxford (pb)	1-85937-411-5	£9.99	West Midlands (pb)	1-85937-289-9	£9.99
Oxfordshire (pb)	1-85937-430-1	£9.99	West Sussex	1-85937-148-5	£14.99
Peak District (pb)	1-85937-280-5	£9.99	West Yorkshire (pb)	1-85937-201-5	£9.99
Penzance	1-85937-069-1	£12.99	Weymouth (pb)	1-85937-209-0	£9.99
Peterborough (pb)	1-85937-219-8	£9.99	Wiltshire (pb)	1-85937-277-5	£9.99
Piers	1-85937-237-6	£17.99	Wiltshire Churches (pb)	1-85937-171-x	£9.99
Plymouth	1-85937-119-1	£12.99	Wiltshire Living Memories	1-85937-245-7	£14.99
Poole & Sandbanks (pb)	1-85937-251-1	£9.99	Winchester (pb)	1-85937-428-x	£9.99
Preston (pb)	1-85937-212-0	£9.99	Windmills & Watermills	1-85937-242-2	£17.99
Reading (pb)	1-85937-238-4	£9.99	Worcester (pb)	1-85937-165-5	£9.99
Romford (pb)	1-85937-319-4	£9.99	Worcestershire	1-85937-152-3	£14.99
Salisbury (pb)	1-85937-239-2	£9.99	York (pb)	1-85937-199-x	£9.99
Scarborough (pb)	1-85937-379-8	£9.99	Yorkshire (pb)	1-85937-186-8	£9.99
St Albans (pb)	1-85937-341-0	£9.99	Yorkshire Living Memories	1-85937-166-3	£14.99

See Frith books on the internet www.francisfrith.co.uk

FRITH PRODUCTS & SERVICES

Francis Frith would doubtless be pleased to know that the pioneering publishing venture he started in 1860 still continues today. A hundred and forty years later, The Francis Frith Collection continues in the same innovative tradition and is now one of the foremost publishers of vintage photographs in the world. Some of the current activities include:

Interior Decoration

Today Frith's photographs can be seen framed and as giant wall murals in thousands of pubs, restaurants, hotels, banks, retail stores and other public buildings throughout the country. In every case they enhance the unique local atmosphere of the places they depict and provide reminders of gentler days in an increasingly busy and frenetic world.

Product Promotions

Frith products are used by many major companies to promote the sales of their own products or to reinforce their own history and heritage. Frith promotions have been used by Hovis bread, Courage beers, Scots Porage Oats, Colman's mustard, Cadbury's foods, Mellow Birds coffee, Dunhill pipe tobacco, Guinness, and Bulmer's Cider.

Genealogy and Family History

As the interest in family history and roots grows world-wide, more and more people are turning to Frith's photographs of Great Britain for images of the towns, villages and streets where their ancestors lived; and, of course, photographs of the churches and chapels where their ancestors were christened, married and buried are an essential part of every genealogy tree and family album.

Frith Products

All Frith photographs are available Framed or just as Mounted Prints and Posters (size 23 x 16 inches). These may be ordered from the address below. From time to time other products - Address Books, Calendars, Table Mats, etc - are available.

The Internet

Already twenty thousand Frith photographs can be viewed and purchased on the internet through the Frith websites and a myriad of partner sites.

For more detailed information on Frith companies and products, look at these sites:

www.francisfrith.co.uk
www.francisfrith.com
(for North American visitors)

See the complete list of Frith Books at:

www.francisfrith.co.uk

This web site is regularly updated with the latest list of publications from the Frith Book Company. If you wish to buy books relating to another part of the country that your local bookshop does not stock, you may purchase on-line.

For further information, trade, or author enquiries please contact us at the address below:
The Francis Frith Collection, Frith's Barn, Teffont, Salisbury, Wiltshire, England SP3 5QP.
Tel: +44 (0)1722 716 376 Fax: +44 (0)1722 716 881 Email: sales@francisfrith.co.uk

See Frith books on the internet www.francisfrith.co.uk

TO RECEIVE YOUR **FREE** MOUNTED PRINT

Mounted Print
Overall size 14 x 11 inches

Cut out this Voucher and return it with your remittance for £1.95 to cover postage and handling, to UK addresses. For overseas addresses please include £4.00 post and handling. Choose any photograph included in this book. Your SEPIA print will be A4 in size, and mounted in a cream mount with burgundy rule line, overall size 14 x 11 inches.

Order additional Mounted Prints at HALF PRICE (only £7.49 each*)

If there are further pictures you would like to order, possibly as gifts for friends and family, purchase them at half price (no additional postage and handling required).

Have your Mounted Prints framed*

For an additional £14.95 per print you can have your chosen Mounted Print framed in an elegant polished wood and gilt moulding, overall size 16 x 13 inches (no additional postage and handling required).

---

* IMPORTANT!
These special prices are only available if ordered using the original voucher on this page (no copies permitted) and at the same time as your free Mounted Print, for delivery to the same address

---

Frith Collectors' Guild

From time to time we publish a magazine of news and stories about Frith photographs and further special offers of Frith products. If you would like 12 months FREE membership, please return this form.

Send completed forms to:
The Francis Frith Collection, Frith's Barn, Teffont, Salisbury, Wiltshire SP3 5QP

Voucher for **FREE** and Reduced Price Frith Prints

Picture no.	Page number	Qty	Mounted @ £7.49	Framed + £14.95	Total Cost
		1	**Free of charge***	£	£
			£7.49	£	£
			£7.49	£	£
			£7.49	£	£
			£7.49	£	£
			£7.49	£	£

Please allow 28 days for delivery	*** Post & handling**	£1.95
Book Title	**Total Order Cost**	£

Please do not photocopy this voucher. Only the original is valid, so please cut it out and return it to us.

I enclose a cheque / postal order for £ . . . .
made payable to 'The Francis Frith Collection'
OR please debit my Mastercard / Visa / Switch / Amex card
(credit cards please on all overseas orders)

Number . . . .

Issue No(Switch only) . . . . .Valid from (Amex/Switch) . . . .

Expires . . . . Signature . . . .

Name Mr/Mrs/Ms . . . .

Address . . . .

. . . .

. . . . Postcode . . . .

Daytime Tel No . . . . Valid to 31/12/02

The Francis Frith Collectors' Guild

Please enrol me as a member for 12 months free of charge.

Name Mr/Mrs/Ms . . . .

Address . . . .

. . . .

. . . .

. . . . Postcode . . . .

Would you like to find out more about Francis Frith?

We have recently recruited some entertaining speakers who are happy to visit local groups, clubs and societies to give an illustrated talk documenting Frith's travels and photographs. If you are a member of such a group and are interested in hosting a presentation, we would love to hear from you.

Our speakers bring with them a small selection of our local town and county books, together with sample prints. They are happy to take orders. A small proportion of the order value is donated to the group who have hosted the presentation. The talks are therefore an excellent way of fundraising for small groups and societies.

Can you help us with information about any of the Frith photographs in this book?

We are gradually compiling an historical record for each of the photographs in the Frith archive. It is always fascinating to find out the names of the people shown in the pictures, as well as insights into the shops, buildings and other features depicted.

If you recognize anyone in the photographs in this book, or if you have information not already included in the author's caption, do let us know. We would love to hear from you, and will try to publish it in future books or articles.

Our production team

Frith books are produced by a small dedicated team at offices in the converted Grade II listed 18th-century barn at Teffont near Salisbury, illustrated above. Most have worked with the Frith Collection for many years. All have in common one quality: they have a passion for the Frith Collection. The team is constantly expanding, but currently includes:

Jason Buck, John Buck, Douglas Burns, Heather Crisp, Isobel Hall, Rob Hames, Hazel Heaton, Peter Horne, James Kinnear, Tina Leary, Hannah Marsh, Eliza Sackett, Terence Sackett, Sandra Sanger, Shelley Tolcher, Susanna Walker, Clive Wathen and Jenny Wathen.